It's A New Beginning:

How to Turn Setbacks Into Comebacks

WILLIE ALFONSO

IT'S A NEW BEGINNING

How to Turn Setbacks Into Comebacks

WILLIE ALFONSO

Foreword by ALONZO MOURNING

I met Pastor Willie twenty years ago when I was a player for the New York Knicks. His story of new beginnings inspired me to become a better player and coach. Today, if you're searching for your new beginning, or comebacks with your name on it—this book is for you!

—Mark Jackson
ESPN Game Analyst

I have had the privilege of knowing Willie Alfonso for over ten years. I can say with certainty that his life and character testify that Jesus is alive. He is one of the most sincere and authentic people I have come to know. May your heart be transformed from the example of this ordinary servant.

—David Tyree
New York Giants Super Bowl XLII Champion

Willie Alfonso is a man of integrity. What you see is what you get. For the past twenty years, I have gotten to know Pastor Willie as a player for the San Antonio Spurs, and as a coach for the New Jersey/Brooklyn Nets. I appreciate his story, prayers, and the courage it gave me to become a better leader. There is no way you can read his book without envisioning your new beginning.

—Avery Johnson
San Antonio Spurs 1999 NBA Championship
Head Coach for the Alabama Crimson Tide

I've had the privilege of working alongside of Willie Alfonso for twenty years of sports team ministry. His story will inspire, and challenge young and old to believe that God can equip anyone to fulfill His purposes.

—George McGovern
Chaplain of New York Giants
Chapel Leader for the New York Yankees

It's A New Beginning: How to Turn Setbacks Into Comebacks is an incredible story of overcoming the odds. It's more than just a story though, it's a declaration that there's no obstacle, struggle or situation we can't rise above when God is in the picture. The world may say; *three strikes and you're out,* but Willie Alfonso is living proof that modern day miracles do exist. He stands as a trophy of grace encouraging us that victory is within reach. You can always begin again.

—Michael Durso
Senior Pastor, Christ Tabernacle

Who could ever look at the life of Chaplain Willie Alfonso and dare say that God is not alive and well, full of love and is in the restoration business? Only God could have devised a plan to make this poor, homeless, and illiterate child to be one of the greatest influencers of our time. God has given him a unique voice to speak to the poor and downtrodden in the ghetto—as well as to the rich and famous athletic superstars in the world today! *It's A New Beginning* defies all logic, and is living proof that God still uses the *nobodies* according to this worlds standards because they are *some bodies* to Him!

—Maria Durso
Co-Pastor, Christ Tabernacle
Author of *From Your Head to Your Heart*

"Everything that we have—right thinking and right living, a clean slate and a fresh start—comes from God by way of Jesus Christ. That's why we have the saying, 'If you're going to blow a horn, blow a trumpet for God'" (I Corinthians 1:26-31, MSG). Pastor Willie Alfonso's life, ministry and this book is a resounding trumpet for God! May the whole world hear it and be encouraged by the *amazing grace* of *Jesus!*

—Ralph Castillo
Teaching Pastor, Christ Tabernacle

I have known Chaplain Willie for many years and have

heard his story many times. Neither he nor his story cease to amaze me. This story—and the man who lived it—will inspire you to dream for more, pray for more, believe for more and act for more in your life. If Willie can become the man he is, having come from where he came from, then all of us can see our lives through the lens of greater possibility. Read this book and raise your sights for more.

—Terry A. Smith
Lead Pastor, The Life Christian Church, West Orange, New Jersey
Author of *Live 10:Jump-Start the Best Version of Your Life*

During my entire career as a New York Yankee, I have had the privilege of knowing Pastor Willie Alfonso. I am eternally grateful for the wisdom I received from him over the years. Now in his new book, the rest of the world can experience the life and the ministry of a man who has been such a blessing to me. I know a good *closer* when I see one. This book will close the old chapters in your life, and set you up for a new beginning

—Mariano Rivera
#42 Retired Relief Pitcher, New York Yankees

Our backgrounds and stories sound very similar, but we have been placed in different arenas. *It's A New Beginning: How to Turn Setbacks Into Comebacks* captures the way God can take Willie Alfonso from a forgotten, broken child and turn him into a man that influences some of the biggest names in sports history. His story will encourage those who are experiencing setbacks, as well as spur on others to never give up on the ones with the tough exterior.

—Nicky Cruz
Evangelist and Author

Chaplain Willie Alfonso's story is nothing short of a miracle! Read it and you'll be inspired to a new level of faith.

—Jim Cymbala
Senior Pastor, The Brooklyn Tabernacle

In Memory of Otto Lang.

TABLE OF CONTENTS

ACKNOWLEDGMENTS

First to my wife Nancy. We have literally grown up together, and experienced so much together. I love you baby! I look forward to tomorrow because I know you will be by my side.

To the three girls that each stole my heart, my daughters Venus, Yvette and Krista. Venus, as our first born, you were our *experiment*, but if I must say so myself—we did really well! You have become a godly woman, wife, and mother. Thank you for being my assistant and keeping me organized. Thank you to my son in law, Miguel Vasquez, and my two grandchildren Julie and Jonathan.

To Yvette, thank you for the many debates on politics and social issues that we have had. You know how I love a good debate!

To Krista, thank you for being such an example of strength and perseverance. You have had so many challenges, but you continue to learn and grow from them. I have learned a lot with you and from you.

To Ralph Castillo, thank you for your tireless pursuit in helping me find a way to get this book written and published. Thank you for all the time you invested. You are my *familia*.

To Pastors Michael and Maria Durso and our Christ Tabernacle Church family, thank you for your love and support. There is *No Place Like Home!*

To Renee Fisher, thank you for taking me on to get this book written. You were literally God sent. After eating my Puerto Rican food, you are now an honorary NY Rican!

To Gus Sosa and Sally Walker, thank you for being the first positive male role models in my life.

To George McGovern, the NY Yankees organization, Baseball Chapel, and the Brooklyn Nets organization, thank you for allowing me to serve on your teams. What a dream come true!

A special thanks to Nacho and Ĩrma, and the rest of the Nieves family for adopting me into their family when I married Nancy. You have been such an example of how a family goes through good and bad times, but stick together.

A special thanks to our loyal churches, ministries and supporters—including the Mahler, Benson, and Chong families—who have faithfully given to Nancy and I. To John Urban and his family for all the years of supporting inner city kids. Without your generosity, we couldn't do what God has called us to do.

Lastly, to my siblings, I know we've had a lot of setbacks, but I am so proud to say you are my brothers and sisters. I love you all very much. I pray God's blessings on each of you and your families.

FOREWORD

I am thankful to the Reverend Willie Alfonso for being a guiding light in my life. When Pastor Willie showed up in my hospital room and asked me what I was going to do about God, it hit me in a way that no question ever had.

I don't believe it was a coincidence that I signed with the New Jersey—now Brooklyn—Nets and not some other team. I don't believe it was a coincidence that, even though he expected me to brush him off the day after my kidney transplant something drove him to go to the hospital and give me another chance.

I wrote in my book *Resilience* that I didn't know what God's plan was, but it pleased me to be in that position because I knew that this was just the beginning. *It was a new beginning.* By going through what I would have to go through, I would be doing God's work. I would help others get through what they would have to get through because I had gone through it, too.

In *It's A New Beginning*, Pastor Willie shares his incredible life story of growing up in one of the toughest neighborhoods in America. His story of how to turn setbacks into comebacks will inspire you to see *hope* in the midst of devastating circumstances. Each chapter is power packed with questions, like the question he asked me that day in the hospital, to guide you through the book. In its pages, Pastor Willie shows you what I also had to learn—the joy of doing God's work—despite any and all setbacks.

Today, if you're searching for your last comeback like I was—it's still not too late; it's a new beginning!

—Alonzo Mourning
Miami Heat 2006 NBA Championship, NBA Hall of Famer
VP of Player Development, Miami Heat

CHAPTER 1: GROWING UP BROOKLYN

I am a New Yorker. Born and raised. I love my city, and couldn't imagine living anywhere else. However, growing up Brooklyn wasn't exactly easy because there were *nine* of us. I was number three of seven children. I had two brothers and four sisters. We were Puerto Rican and poor. It didn't help that my dad was an alcoholic. Now, I'm not talking about a few drinks every now and then—I'm talkin' *raging* drunk.

And he was abusive. Man was he abusive.

Most people have fond memories of their childhood. I don't. My brothers and sisters and I lived in absolute fear. Even thinking about it gives me the chills. My siblings and I all found different ways to cope when he was drinking. Some of us would hide under the bed. Others wouldn't talk much for fear they might set dad off. Even cooking sounds coming from the kitchen made him angry. We didn't *dare* do or say anything to trigger a tirade. Some days I went without supper so I could hide in my room after I got home from William Floyd PS 59 Elementary School in Brooklyn on Throop and Park Ave.

My earliest childhood memory was a nightly routine that included my dresser, cans of 7-UP, and whatever else I could find in my room. Every night, I pushed my dresser up against the back of my bedroom door with as much strength as I could muster. I secured the dresser firmly underneath the door handle until it locked in place.

Click.

I emptied out a sack of 7-UP cans on my bedroom floor and placed the most ragged ones close enough to the edge. One by one, I placed them on top of the dresser. Mostly, I used whatever I had lying around in my room before going to bed. Sometimes I'd place plastic toy soldiers on top of each can so they packed a powerful punch when they hit the floor together. When my dad stumbled home drunk from whatever social club or bar he was at drinking at with his buddies—I was ready. The loud sounds woke me up.

Crash!

Bang!

Clink!

The noise of the cans hitting the floor gave me enough time to run out as *fast* as I could before my dad forced himself in the room. The second those cans rattled and scattered all over the floor—I was out of there. No matter how crusty my eyes were or how sore my body was from the previous day's beating, I got up. I made—no I *forced*—my legs to run as fast as my body would carry me out of the room and away from his grasp. Sometimes he would catch me or one of my brothers or sisters. As much as I loved my siblings—and I *did* love them—I couldn't sacrifice another body part. My dad didn't know the meaning of *no* or *stop*. I had to be concerned with me, numero-uno, because no one else was going to.

Not even my mom!

Looking back, that's probably *the* reason why I became such a fast runner. My dad taught me how to run, and certainly not in a good way.

DYSFUNCTION REIGNED

The Miriam-Webster Dictionary defines dysfunction as *the condition of having poor and unhealthy behaviors and attitudes within a group of people.*[1] I didn't know they had a term for my family growing up in Brooklyn until I read it. That was us. The Alfonso family lived in absolute fear of dad.

From a young age, I had no one to look up to. I relied on no one else, but me. My dad never told me he loved me, and neither did my mom. I learned how to go from Plan A to Plan B to Plan C…to Plan Z on a dime. I developed survival skills, and learned how to cope inside the apartment when my dad was home. When my father wasn't drinking, he didn't talk a whole lot. He worked as a merchant seaman and would be gone for *d-a-y-s* at a time. Sometimes, he was gone for weeks at a time. While he was away, time felt like my only respite from the pain he inflicted on *all* of us. I'm not sure what was worse: the psychological, emotional, or physical pain I endured.

At least the pain went away eventually, *right?*

The days and the nights passed quicker when my dad was on the ship. By the time he was back, my bruises had disappeared and my bones were almost straight. However, he was never gone long enough for my mind to heal.

I never stopped worrying.

I worried about the next time my dad would grab me or my siblings. We shared a tiny 5 bedroom apartment on 260 Ellery Street not too far from the Williamsburg Bridge. It felt like someone placed pins and needles on the floor because my feet never touched the ground. I was always tiptoeing around him. If I stayed too long—something bad was bound to happen. I was always glancing at the back of the apartment door *just in case* my dad came swinging right through it. Just when I thought it was safe—dysfunction reigned and his name was *dad*.

GET OUTTA' HERE

I often found mom lighting incense and saying curses under her breath about people who crossed her. If you didn't want to make my dad angry—you *definitely* didn't want to cross mom, otherwise she'd put a curse on you. If you really upset her, she'd curse your family too, and all your living relatives. She had a shrine in the house that nobody was allowed to touch but her. She lit candles and spent a lot of time praying to the dead. I thought it was creepy, but I never said anything.

Mom never put up a fight with my dad. How could she? She was too busy taking care of herself, us kids, or taking another beating from him. I'm not surprised she never left him to take us to live with my Uncle Frank. There was no such thing as single parent households in the 1950's or

1960's. No matter how bad it got, she would *never* call the cops—that would have fueled my dad's anger even more. Instead, she lit incense and prayed.

When I was about six or seven years old, I came home from school one day to find my mom doing laundry—a rare sight. Washing machines and dryers didn't exist yet. My mom waited until the laundry piled up just enough to make my dad angry, but not angry enough to give her a beating. Since she had to wash each piece by hand, and hang them dry on the line outside our apartment—she rarely did laundry. If the weather was awful, forget it! It's a good thing we were poor because we didn't have many clothes to wear anyway. If mom didn't wash your clothes or make your food—you went *without*. No laundry meant no clean clothes. Sometimes I'd wear the same old raggedy t-shirt until I got a new one. And by *got* I mean *stole*.

One particular day in the spring when the snow melted, and the weather was warm enough to hang the clothes outside of our first floor apartment to dry—I watched mom do the laundry. She grabbed the laundry basket, and headed for the window. She must have been distracted because she didn't hear my dad come up behind her.

Dad was home, and he was drunk *again*.

The noise she made must have made him angry because he snuck up from behind her. He pretended to push her out the window. I heard her booming laugh as she dusted off his hands to finish hanging the laundry. Unfortunately, he didn't let her. Before she could turn her back on him, dad put his hands on the small of her back. With one push—she went flying out of the first floor window. My dad literally shoved my mom out of the apartment!

I froze.

I could feel my heart beating in my chest. I wanted to run and check on my mom.

Was she okay?

Was she hurt?

4

I didn't dare make a sound. I didn't dare let my dad see me afraid. He could smell fear man. My dad preyed on fear. It made him feel bigger than everybody else. It didn't matter that his six foot frame towered over us anyway.

I could smell my dad's drunken rage turn and focus on *me*. That's when I heard it. My mom's scream. The terror in her voice. If I moved a muscle, my dad might throw me out of the window too. I could feel my knees shaking like trees under me. I prayed to God I didn't faint.

I needed to get outta' here. But how?

I'd never been more afraid in my entire life. I think my lips turned purple because I stopped breathing. It's like what you see on the cartoons when the character's eyes come out of their head, and their heart bursts through their chest. That was me. Everything turned into slow motion. I could hear my dad yelling down at my mom.

Be quiet, he said. Then he turned and looked right at me. *Who's next?*

I ran right past him and didn't even bother to check on mom. I kept running until I reached the J Train. That was the day I knew something was wrong. Really wrong. From that day forward I vowed *never* to step foot inside of the apartment from sunup to sundown. Every day, I got up early for school and practically ran out of the apartment. It didn't matter how hungry I was after school—or if it was snowing outside—I *always* found a place to go and hang out with my friends until sunset. As soon as it turned dark, I raced home.

In Brooklyn, there was an unspoken rule parents had—or should I say—*all* New Yorkers abided by. As long as you were home before the glow of the street lights—you were okay. I'm a fast runner, but some days the lights messed with me. I swear they weren't on timers because the sinister lights on *my* street always turned on at different times, as if they created the whole plot to make the children live in fear of their parents. In the summer, the lights would *still* come on when it was light because they weren't programmed for daylight savings time. The street light trumped the sunlight.

You're gonna get it, they'd say mockingly.

Get outta here, I said.

As long as I made it into the apartment before the street lights came on, I could rest easy. I lived to regret days I didn't make it home in time. *How* I made it home was beyond me. Every muscle in my body hurt so bad from my dad throwing me against the wall, or beating me with his belt as I huffed it home. It was all I could do to put one leg in front of the other. My lungs burned. I though I was going to pass out. My toes were all blistery from the shoes that I had outgrown the year—or two—before. By the time I reached the apartment, my face was hot, my palms were sweaty, and I reeked of B.O.

I could hear the screams of the kids on my block who *didn't* make it home on time. No matter how sorry they were—their parents beat them like mine. I couldn't wince because I had to be home in a New York minute or I was going to get the same beat down! It was excruciating to hear my friends—kids even younger than me—being beat on by their dads and moms. *What* kind of fathers and mothers beat their kids until they were black and blue?

Don't answer that.

MY HOME WASN'T SAFE

I was living in a hell hole. Back then, there was *no such thing* as child abuse. Parents spanked their kids when they disobeyed. If they didn't get home before the street lights turned on—they got a whooping. And sometimes parents beat their kids for absolutely no reason at all. Some of my friends were forced to kneel on top of rice on the wood floor until their knees and legs bled from all the squirming. That was just normal. Back then, parents did whatever they wanted to do to their kids.

My dad would just *beat* us.

Hard.

He would hit us until we were black and blue with his weapon of choice: the belt. He was a merchant seaman, and he had a *special* belt with ball bearings on the end of it—and by special—I mean it hurt like hell. It didn't matter whether he hit us in the face, back, butt, hands, or feet. He whipped us until we were black and blue. No amount of crying, pleading, begging, screaming or squirming deterred him from hitting us harder. No matter if I had a black eye, a welt, or a broken bone—I healed at home. I didn't know which was worse, getting beat by my dad or staying home from school the next day knowing my dad was still home and *still* drunk.

That never stopped him though. That wound on my finger? Reopened! That black eye I just got? Another shade of purple! Sometimes I didn't go to school for weeks at a time because you didn't kiss and tell. Each time he hit me, I lost a piece of my soul. But I never let him see me break.

I've heard people say scars are the tattoos of the brave. I disagree. My body was covered from head to toe, and I never once felt brave. My home wasn't safe. I just wanted to be loved. I wanted to be a normal kid who went to school, got along with his family, and ate three square meals a day. I didn't *dare* show up at school or go the hospital unless I was dying—I'll get to *that* story in the next chapter.

Because I missed so many days of school, I never learned how to read. Just because I didn't know how to read, didn't mean I was *stupid*. I wasn't. There were plenty of times I thought my body was broken beyond repair. That broken finger? I made my own splint! That blackish-purplish eye? I wore a hat!

Lucky for me, I wasn't the only sibling who stayed home from school. Safety in numbers, right? Sometimes we hid together or left the house to find a place to hide—that is, if we had the strength to make it out of the apartment. My dad's *other* weapon of choice was a spoon. When he didn't feel like whipping out his ball-bearing merchant seaman belt, he beat us with a giant iron spoon. He was a cook on the ship, and he brought his spoons home just to torture us. I *still* have marks on my body from those spoons. To this day, I prefer to eat with a fork.

THE MOST TERRIFYING DAY

Unfortunately, that wasn't the *worst* of it. I came home from school to witness the *most* terrifying day of my life. My dad was wielding an ax.

Yes, you read that right.

An *ax*.

I pinned my body behind the door so he wouldn't grab me. He was a new level of drunk than I had ever seen before. He was tearing up the house with murderous intentions. In his drunken rage, he axed the dinning room table to pieces along with all my mom's dishes. Once they crashed to the floor—I ran. I honestly don't remember much else after that. I ran out as fast as I could.

By then, I was good at two things: running and finding hiding spots. Name a borough in New York City, and I'll tell you where to hide. I hid in an abandoned building for *at least* a couple of days after that day to give my dad the chance to calm down—that, or go back on the ship.

THE DAY I BECAME A MAN

When I came home from the most terrifying day—something inside me *broke*. I resolved in my heart that one day I would stand up to my dad. I wasn't sure when or how—but I would. I couldn't live like this anymore. All the abuse and fear made me feel like a caged animal.

Enough was enough.

I remember rehearsing in front of the bathroom mirror what I wanted to say to my father before school. After school, I hid myself behind the dresser to rehearse. With each can of 7-Up that I placed on my dresser, I practiced what I wanted to say. I knew words weren't enough to change his mind. I would need to use force against force. Should I channel John Wayne and point my finger in his face like a pretend gun while saying, *I won't be wronged. I won't be insulted. I won't be laid a-hand on. I don't do these things to other people, and I require the same from [you dad]*.[2]

Or maybe I should I protest like Martin Luther King

Junior and ask my brothers and sisters to protest with me? I rehearsed what I might *do* until I actually had the courage to act. My only problem was that I wasn't an actor. I was just a ten year old kid trying to survive growing up Brooklyn.

The day I hit my dad was the day I became a man.

I don't remember what my parents were arguing about in particular. I *do* remember, however, finding the courage to take a deep breath. I stepped in front of my mom in time to stop my dad's fist.

Slap.

It was the slap heard around the world. Gone were all the words I had rehearsed.

Punch.

In one fell swoop, I leaned in with my right fist and punched him in the face and knocked him off his feet. He wasn't expecting to be hit. Nobody, I mean *n-o-b-d-y* ever stood up to my father. Since he didn't brace himself, he flew about a foot in the air before hitting the hardwood floor.

Boom.

I had won.

In his humiliation, my dad ran out of the apartment. This time it was *him* running—not me. This time it was *him* who stayed away for a few days—not me.

To my surprise, I thought my mom would thank me for stopping him from punching her in the face. She didn't. I thought my brothers and sisters would be grateful because somebody had finally put an end to his beatings. They weren't. Instead of smelling my dad's intoxicated breath, the apartment smelled like the stench of fear from my mother, brothers and sisters. The fear was so thick it blanketed our apartment like incense. It was intoxicating, and not in a good way.

My dad's phone call broke the silence. A few days later, he reappeared from my Aunt's flower shop down the street and told my mom he wanted to come home.

My dad gave my mom a choice: live with him or me—
she couldn't choose both. My mother looked at me with
glazed eyes and said,

Pack your things.

She choose *him.*

I was eleven years old the day I became a man.

You might be thinking your story isn't as crazy as mine, but it doesn't matter. I want you to keep an eye out for patterns and similarities. Sometimes it takes another person's story to help you understand your past, and what makes your story unique. You can answer these questions for yourself as well as in a small group setting (see page 94). My goal is for you to be able to look back on your life and see the setbacks along with the comebacks. Please take a few minutes and answer the questions below before moving on to Chapter 2 in *It's A New Beginning: How to Turn Setbacks Into Comebacks.*

QUESTIONS

1. Where did you grow up?
2. What was your family like? Home life?
3. Do you have any sad childhood memories? Happy? Why or why not?
4. At what age did you become a man or a woman? What happened?

CHAPTER 2: THAT'S *YOUR* SON!

If Growing up Brooklyn was a hellhole, my nightmare had *just* begun. The sinister streetlamps no longer taunted me in the evening or called my name. The streets were my home now! However, their presence wasn't exactly welcoming. There was no mat. No protection from the elements. I had no one to tuck me in at night or wake me up for school in the morning—not that I ever had that living at home.

My Uncle Frank lived on Blake and Alabama in Brooklyn. I asked if I could live with him. He owned a refrigerator company and was gone during the day. He said yes, but *only* if I promised to go to school the next day. He didn't want me goofing off at his place during the day while he was at work.

Since I needed a meal and somewhere warm to stay for the night, I agreed. Every night I slept under the bed in fear. I never knew when bullets would come flying through the apartment. Growing up Brooklyn, that kind of thing was normal. The neighborhoods were so hot. They were filled with crime. It was either live with Uncle Frank or live on the street. It was a nice arrangement for a while—even if I *did* have to attend school the next day.

William Floyd PS 59 Elementary School was always under construction. Back then, schools didn't shut down for a remodel. They stayed open. They also didn't post any signs warning the students. They had caution cones. I didn't let that stop me.

As an adventurous kid—I made a game out of jumping over the cones with my friends. During recess, we would jump when the teacher wasn't looking, and climb on top of the metal beams. As long as we didn't see any construction workers, we would climb pretty high until we could see the wooden planks supporting new floors and elevators. We loved running along the beams. Sometimes we'd even play tag. It was all fun and games until someone got hurt.

Me.

One of pieces of lumber wasn't secured as tightly as I thought. When I ran across it—it came flying loose and landed on top of my left foot—crushing it.

Ouch!

I was stuck. I could tell my foot was injured pretty bad so I yelled for help. That's when they left. All of them. I'm pretty sure my friends were afraid they were going to get in trouble. One of us was *always* in the principal's office. I'm not surprised they ran away—because I would have done the same. Thankfully, I didn't have to wait too long.

The principal heard my yells and called the paramedics. They took me to Cumberland hospital on Portland Avenue in Brooklyn. I waited in the Emergency Room for *h-o-u-r-s* before one of the doctors looked at my foot. He took one look at me, my foot, and the nurse—and said it didn't look good. I needed surgery right away. I would have to stay the weekend. A nurse asked for my parents information, and I gave her my mom's number because I didn't have Uncle Frank's memorized.

I was crushed.

But not for any reasons you might think. I was *used* to pain. My dad inflicted so much physical pain on me that I eventually learned to take it. I knew my foot would heal. I was more upset about missing the World's Fair in Flushing Meadows Corona Park. Besides, all my friends would be there. It was *the* thing to do in New York.

More than fifty million people from all around the world were camped out in my backyard, but I couldn't participate. There was a twelve-story unisphere that looked like a globe built to represent all the nations represented at the Fair. In fact, it *still* exists to this day including the ruins from the New York State Pavilion.

The World's Fair was such a big deal because it had been years since the last one was hosted. I heard about the 1939 and 1940 Worlds Fair from my parents, Aunt, and my Uncle Frank. The stories they told were amazing. They told me how fun it was when they were growing up. Only this time, so much had changed.

I was crushed to be missing out. I heard NASA built a replica of a spaceship that I was dying to see. I didn't get to see it. While everyone was enjoying the massive exhibits from different countries and businesses around the world—I was stuck inside the hospital all by myself. I could only dream of walking through each one of the pavilions while I sat in my hospital bed growing more and more depressed.

I was so lonely.

No one came to visit me in the hospital. None of my friends, siblings, or my even my parents. I thought my mom would for sure visit me, but she didn't.

Not *one* person visited me in the hospital.

It was the longest two weeks of my life. I could only hear about what was happening at the World's Fair through the nurses, but they were too busy working. By the time my parents were called again—it was too late. I had missed the Fair. They only came to pick me up because they *had* to sign a release form so I could leave.

LIVIN' ON THE STREETS

My parents picked me up at the hospital only to drop me off at my Uncle Frank's. I was used to feeling abandoned. I knew I had to learn how to survive if I was going to make it to my next birthday or *any* birthday. From 8 AM to 7 PM, I ran the streets. No one forced me to be home before the street lights. I had nothing but the street lights to guide me. No one, not even my Uncle Frank, forced me to attend school. At first, I liked my new found freedom because of my accident. I didn't care about going back to school—but I knew I needed to learn how to fend for myself. Unfortunately, stealing was the *only* way I knew how to survive.

If I was hungry—I *stole*.

If I needed something to wear—I *stole*.

If I needed something—I *had* to figure a way.

Hustling was my middle name. I didn't know all the rules of the streets yet, but I would soon figure out that only the strong survived. For instance, New York City loved their morning bagels. And so did I. Street vendors, delis, and bakeries *all* sold bagels. I choose to grab-and-run from the street vendors because it was easy access. Plus, the tourists were a great distraction. I could smell tourists forming a mile away. While they huddled together in their warm outfits and gloves for their slice of NYC, I easily outsmarted the vendors. As long as I didn't steal from the same vendor twice, I ate bagels for breakfast.

It wasn't as easy to grab a drink though.

I loved 7-Up, which is probably why I had collected so many cans at my parent's house. But this was no time to be picky. Sometimes I went thirsty, or hungry—or both. When vendors saw me coming, I ran even faster. No matter how much my left foot hurt from the accident—I kept running.

It was quite an ordeal every morning to find a hot breakfast, but the grumbling sounds in my stomach kept me going. It was either that or eat from the garbage cans on the streets. The vendors had to man their cart otherwise someone smarter, taller, or faster than me would clean them out when they weren't looking.

During the day, I missed my friends. Since no one was forcing me to go to school, I didn't go regularly. I knew if I went back, the teachers would just send me straight to the principal's office for missing so much school. And I was already in a lot of trouble with the principal since he's the one that found me when I fell and crushed my left foot. I was too embarrassed to tell my teachers I was homeless, they would have thought I was lying or worse—called my parents. So I stayed away.

I entertained myself by finding new places to hang out. There was always something going on in New York City, things to do, or people to watch. During the night, I begged my friends to sneak me into their rooms. Sometimes I'd have to tip toe up multiple floors of creaky apartment stairs without getting caught. When I'd get to the door, I would knock once, softly, giving my friends the signal to distract their parents long enough for me to sneak inside. When I didn't sleep at a friend's house, I slept on the streets.

Homeless people weren't very friendly to me. If I picked the wrong abandoned building, I might be harassed or beat up—or worse. I found most homeless men and women to be indifferent though. We were all looking out for ourselves. So was I.

My legs were my only ally. They carried me quickly away from anyone who could do me harm. I also ran far away from anyone who might try to arrest me. I had to be careful so that I might not attract unwanted attention from the police.

Jail was *n-o-t* an option.

My biggest fear was getting sent back to my parents house since I was a minor. My mother made it pretty clear; I was no longer welcome in the Alfonso apartment. And my father? Well, he was a coward. I didn't care to see *either* of them again.

As long as I evaded my teachers or the cops—it was a good day. If my punishment for standing up to my dad was livin' on the streets, then I wanted to be *the* man on the streets!

THE MAN ON THE STREETS

My father never showed me what being a real man looked like. I didn't want to become like him, so I did whatever I thought was best at the time. Depending on the seasons in New York, I found different places to live. If it was summer time—I slept in an abandoned building or a park.

Central Park was my favorite. It was large enough that I never got caught. I ran until the only sound I heard was my labored breath and my feet hitting the pavement. Then, I'd find the nearest park bench to sleep under, which offered minimal protection in case it rained.

In the wintertime, I noticed homeless people tended to commit the most crime—or should I say—get *caught* for their crimes. Instead of spending the freezing winter outside in the elements—they were guaranteed a warm bed with three square meals a day in city jail. Maybe they thought they were being street smart, but I didn't buy it.

I had never been to jail, and I didn't plan to any time soon. I was too smart to get caught. I *always* found a way. I could turn on a dime. If plans changed—I rolled with it. I went from Plan A to Plan Z without a second thought, if I needed to. I only stole what I needed to survive. And I could run away fast. I knew how to climb fences, jump from building to building, and even *into* a building if I needed to. I jumped fences—even the kind with electrical wires on top.

Nothing phased me.

The cops were always looking to catch neighborhood thieves so I had to be careful not to steal from one particular block for too long before going on to another. I didn't want the cops knowing who I was, otherwise it was only a matter of time before you had a record and served time in jail. I needed to remain a mystery if I was to survive as *the* man on the streets.

I remember waiting for my friends to get out of school. It was fall in New York City, and the shop owners put out their best winter apparel to attract new customers. I have a lot of respect for New York City shop owners. They're beasts!

How they always kept one eye on the front of the store was a gift. If I wasn't careful, I knew I'd get caught. I *needed* a new coat. Really bad. Nights were getting colder, and the few things I actually owned were back at my parents house. I'm sure my dad had already thrown all of my things in the trash during one of his drunken fits of rage.

So I improvised.

I walked through Manhattan until I settled on a shop on Delancey Street who, I thought, had the best display of men's coats inside the window. My friends would all be impressed if I was wearing one of those bad boys. Delancey Street was riskier than Times Square because there weren't *as many* tourists, but I didn't care. I knew my dark skin would give me away, but I was able to walk inside without being spotted. I immediately walked over to the coats until I found one that I wanted. The second I pulled the coat off the rack—a woman in the store spotted me.

Stop or I'm going to call the police, she yelled.

Without looking at her—I grabbed the coat and ran out of the store as fast as I could. I ran all the way up Delancey Street to Rivington and Norfolk. Now I was hungry *and* thirsty. Before I found a street vendor to steal food from, I put the coat on and sank into the inner lining. I was still hot from running, but I didn't care. Gone was the summer humidity. From now on, if it rained or snowed—I would be warm at night. I only wore it on for a few minutes before I found a place to hide it. People living on the streets were both mean *and* shifty. I didn't trust anybody. I also didn't want anyone stealing my new coat, so I stashed it.

THE J TRAIN

I started doing drugs after my mom kicked me out of the house. My friends and I had a favorite hang out spot in Central Park. We would sneak on to the J Train and ride it over the Williamsburg Bridge into Manhattan. By the time we got off the train—we were high. We sniffed glue, smoked pot, and drank wine.

I quit sniffing glue because it gave me headaches. I only drank wine because my friends were drinking. I told myself that I would *never* abuse alcohol like my father. I was *the* man on the streets now, remember?

The streets will do that to you. There were no rules. They made me feel invincible. I was constantly watching my back because I never knew *if* or when I might get caught. I never did.

Wine was harder to steal so I scored pot from the wannabe thugs who trolled the schools. Each day, after my friends got out of school, we smoked pot and took the J Train into Manhattan. If you were a punk—you couldn't hang with us. We waited for the train cars to come to a stop at Marcy Avenue. Then, one-by-one we'd climb on top of the train cars.

With the most amazing view of New York City, we jumped from car to car as it sped across the Williamsburg Bridge. Life couldn't get any better!

That's when I was offered acid.

Suddenly marijuana didn't seem cool anymore. They called it Sunshine—and it was *everywhere*. We went on acid trips all the time. It felt like we were running on sunshine from sunup to sundown. When it was time to go back to Brooklyn, we'd jump down in between the subway cars before entering the tunnel again at Delancey Street.

Sometimes we did acid.

Sometimes we did pot.

Sometimes we drank wine.

Whatever we had—we used. My Uncle Frank had a lot of used refrigerators laying around from his business. While he thought I was at school—I had my friends all come over. We were playing hooky while he was at work. One of us quickly figured out how to use a wrench to get high with Freon 12 gas from the refrigerators.

QUIT MONKEYING AROUND

I often waited for my friends to get out of JHS 33 Mark Hopkins Junior High School, at a nearby playground. There were usually kids of all ages crawling all over them, so no one noticed I wasn't in school. Most New York City playgrounds were typically equipped with monkey bars, a slide, and a couple of swings. The monkey bars were my favorite for building upper body strength. My legs were already toned, muscular, and fast. And built. Also, I might have loved to impress the girls.

Her name was Lisa.

I never actually spoke to her. I overheard her friends call out her name while they were playing jump rope. Lisa was pretty. She had a lot of freckles, and her bell bottoms bounced with each jump of the rope. While I looked in her direction, I decided to show off my swinging skills. I jumped up to grab the first monkey bar.

Slip.

I noticed, right way, my hands were particularly sweaty. I didn't get nervous easily, so it must have been from the 7-Up can I was drinking earlier. I tried to do a trick so it didn't look like I was falling. I tried jumping two monkey bars at a time so I would have time to wipe my hands on my t-shirt. Instead of catching the next monkey bar, I fell and hit my head on the ground.

I don't remember anything after that.

Someone must have called the paramedics because my body went lifeless. I ended up in the hospital *again*. This time, they took me to The Brooklyn Hospital. I woke up eight days later from a coma.

The doctors said *I* was a miracle.

I was shocked. I couldn't believe that I had survived multiple beatings from my dad, my left foot accidentally getting crushed, and now this?

And for what?

Three weeks later, the doctor asked me again where my parents were and *why* they hadn't come to see me at all. I pretended to swallow real hard like I couldn't answer. I *didn't* want to answer. They never did come to see me when I was in the hospital before, *why* would they visit me now?

I knew the drill.

When my parents were called to sign a release form, I spoke up instead of remaining silent.

Where were you? I asked. *Did you know that I hit my head? Did you care I was in a coma, and that I almost died?*

We were hosting a party at the house, my parents said.

I don't even remember which parent told me. I was steaming mad. I didn't want them to drop me off at Uncle Frank's apartment, but what choice did I have? I didn't live with them anymore. I was too tired to walk.

THAT'S *YOUR* SON!

After my parents dropped me off at Uncle Frank's apartment, I left. I found my friends hanging out in Central Park. They offered me some acid and I gladly got high. My head still hurt, and I couldn't stop hearing their words over and over in my head.

They were hosting a party at the house. Didn't they care about me? Didn't they care that I almost died?

I didn't want to think about what had just happened. When my friends pointed at my head, I showed them the bump—another battle scar. I told them I had been in a coma. They thought it was cool. I didn't. I was tired of getting beat up while livin' on the streets. No matter where I went, trouble followed me. I couldn't catch a break living in the hellhole that was my parents apartment in livin' on the streets in Brooklyn.

But where else was I going to go?

I had no one else to take care of me. It was getting dark, so we decided to ride the J Train back to Brooklyn. Nobody asked me where I was staying for the night. They all knew.

When we reappeared above ground, we spotted a company truck that used to pay us in nickels and dimes to unload their materials used in a coat factory. Not that I ever got to wear any of their coats—I was forced to steal mine. But if we ever saw the truck around town, we could hitch a ride. It was an unspoken rule, and sometimes it saved us from walking a few blocks. Once the truck reached its stop, we'd jump off. A free ride is a free ride, right?

When I hopped on, I felt the wind in my face. Then I felt it. Something I'd never felt before. *Hope.* I was certain my luck was going to change. If I could survive a coma—I could survive anything.

The driver swung a left on Ellery street. That's when I spotted him—my dad. I saw him out of the corner of my eye at Ellery Social Club. He must have gone straight from the hospital to party with his friends. Go figure.

Look at those animals on the truck. Where are those kids parents? My dad yelled.

I was devastated. He must've not seen me. Before I could respond, I heard one of my dad's friend.

Hey! That's your son on the truck!

That's when he saw me. We locked eyes and I gave him the death stare. Of all the things my dad could have said. He looked visibly mortified and embarrassed. I didn't care.

He got up, picked up a chair from the establishment, and started running after the truck. My friends started laughing but I knew better. My dad chased me down until the truck came to a complete stop at a stoplight just so he could hit me over the head with a chair.

The same head that was just injured.

The same head that put me in a coma.

What kinds of traumatic experiences did you have growing up? As you continue reading, it's important to answer the questions below honestly to get the most out of this book. Please take a few minutes and answer the questions below, before moving on to Chapter 3 in *It's A New Beginning: How to Turn Setbacks Into Comebacks*.

QUESTIONS
1. Have you ever stolen? Why or why not?
2. Have you ever done drugs? How old were you when you started?
3. Were you ever hurt by a family members actions growing up? What happened?
4. What's the worst thing anyone's ever said to you?

CHAPTER 3: THE DAY I BECAME NANCY'S PARTNER

The streets were cruel man. I couldn't handle it anymore. The thought that I might not make it to my next birthday traumatized me. I prided myself in being clean. It killed me that my clothes were weeks old. I smelled badly from not showering in months. My teeth were rotten from eating out of trash cans. The police knew my name in almost every neighborhood in Brooklyn.

But I'm a Brooklyn Boy. Where else was I going to go?

Sniffing glue and Freon 12 didn't satisfy any longer. I was angry at myself for drinking cheap wine. I saw how alcohol ruined the lives of my dad, his dad, and grand dad—not to mention our family.

I didn't see any way out. What choice did I have but to forget the pain of my past? Smoking pot didn't sooth me or take away the loneliness. Acid didn't comfort me. Tripping on sunshine was no longer enough, so I turned to harder drugs like heroin and cocaine. I was angry at the world. So angry.

Why did life treat me this way? Why was I dealt this deck of cards?

I knew if I continued to steal and do drugs—I would end up in jail. I did not want to spend the rest of my life behind bars. My Uncle Frank let me continue to live with him, but the older I got—I wanted my own place.

My relationship with my parents was still strained. I never respected my mom for staying with my dad when he beat the living daylights out of her, when he pushed her out of the window, and *especially* when he made her choose between living with him or me.

My mom had reached her bottom—so she said—but I didn't care. I heard from my kid brother that My Uncle Isaul was visiting from Puerto Rico. He was staying with my parents so he could visit the VA hospital in Brooklyn. He was staying with my parents when *it* happened.

My brother said that my dad accused mom of cheating on him with Uncle Isaul. When they both denied cheating on him, he attacked them. He stabbed my uncle and cut open my mom from the top of her left shoulder all the way down to the palm of her hand.

He left her for dead.

If my brother hadn't found her in the hallway outside of the apartment, he said, she would have died. When he found her humped over bleeding, he tied up her arm as quick as he could before calling the paramedics.

At that time, my family was living in a fifth story apartment building. It was a total miracle she survived all the blood loss. She ended up in the hospital with fifteen hundred stitches and a giant scar.

Honestly, I had already stopped listening to my brother. I didn't care. I didn't want to hear any more about my mom and her gruesome story, or that my dad was divorcing her for another woman.

If she was looking for pity or understanding—she wasn't going to get it from me. I wasn't going to call her or come visit her. I couldn't stand to look at her for what she had done to me when she told me to pack my bags.

She never told me that she loved me. She never apologized or asked me for my forgiveness. She never came to visit me in the hospital.

Why should I visit her in the hospital?

I was thankful that my Uncle Frank let me stay at his apartment, but I needed a job. But where? I was barely in high school and not yet legal to work. I knew my choices were limited. Thankfully, it didn't take long until I found someone who would hire me. One of Uncle Frank's customers who lived across the street owned a grocery store.

They called him *Nacho*.

His family owned Grocery Store #14 on Reid Avenue and Kosciusko Street. Right away we hit it off. He had three boys and four girls like my family. They were also Puerto Rican.

Nacho took a chance on me.

He let me stock the shelves during the day and sleep in the basement at night. Unlike Uncle Frank, he didn't make me go to school. He let me eat the food in his store because I worked for it.

I thought I had won the lottery!

The first night I slept in the basement I heard the sound of rats chattering around me. I tried not to peek, but I couldn't help myself. Sure enough, the rats were as big as my fist—almost as big as the rats from the abandoned buildings I used to sleep in. I'm just glad they didn't bite my feet and wake me up like the others.

This time—the rats left me alone. Maybe it was because I no longer feared them. Whatever the reason was—I was just thankful to have a roof over my head. During the day I stocked the shelves, cleaned the store, or whatever Nacho needed me to do. At night, I slept in the grocery store basement.

I quickly earned his trust.

In Puerto Rican culture, the mother is typically *very* protective. Nacho's wife, Îrma, didn't let anyone near her daughters. I respected their family so much—especially since I didn't have one anymore. I remember the day Îrma was planning a Sweet 16 for their daughter Nancy. It was going to be a huge party in the neighborhood. Everyone was dressing up to celebrate Nancy, including a ceremony, dancing, and food—lots of food like rice and beans, and pork chops. Puerto Ricans sure know how to cook! If God would have made me a different race or religion that didn't allow me to eat pork—I don't think I would have survived. I love me some pork!

I never spoke with Nancy until her mother asked me to go to her Sweet 16. Nancy needed an escort and a dance partner. I'm not sure *why* her mom trusted me. Maybe it was because Nacho trusted me. Or maybe it was because I was a year younger than Nancy. One thing I knew is that Irma didn't trust just *anyone* to be her partner. When she asked me, I knew it was a *big* deal.

For the first time in my life, I was conflicted. I was too proud to ask for money, but something in me told me to ask Irma anyway. She agreed and offered to rent me a tux. I couldn't wait to try it on.

Let me tell you—I clean up good!

I had never worn anything that fancy before. They even let me shower upstairs. I remember coming out of the bathroom and walking into their living room feeling like a new man. When I laid eyes on Nancy for the first time I just—*knew*. She looked so beautiful in her mint green dress. For a brief moment, I felt like I was living in a fairy tale, and I'm not a fairy tale kind of guy.

Growing up Brooklyn, my mentality was that only the strong survive. I had to figure out everything by myself—for myself. I had no family. No one to care for me. But, I always found a way—I had to if I wanted to survive.

The first time Nancy and I spoke face-to-face was at her party. We walked down the block to the Luis Social Club her parents rented for the occasion. I opened the door for her while offering my arm. As we walked into the basement, I was so glad she was wearing gloves because I didn't want her to feel the sweat coming from under my arm in my rented tux.

I was so nervous. I honestly don't remember what the first thing was that I said to her. I'm sure I fumbled over my words. In that moment, being a part of their family caught me off guard. It didn't help that Nancy's dark brown eyes saw right through me. She looked at me like no one had ever looked at me before.

My heart was hopeful and yet so afraid from the millions of billions of walls I had built around it from being abandoned by every close family member I had ever known.

I didn't want to get hurt *again*.

Even though I didn't feel worthy of being her partner—I didn't let that stop me. Her kindness drew me closer to her. The smell of her hair, the soft touch of her hand on my arm. We slow danced to the song *Ooh Baby, Baby* by Smokey Robinson and The Miracles. The words leaped from the speakers into my heart. The words rang in my mind as I held her in my arms.

> *Ooh, baby baby*
> *Ooh, baby baby*
> *I'm just about at the end of my rope*
> *But I can't stop trying, I can't give up hope*
> *'Cause I feel that one day, I'll hold you near*[3]

I appreciated being a part of someone's family—even if it was just for a day. I played the part of the prince—I mean partner—as well as I could. The day I became Nancy's partner, I was challenged to think differently about family. It was like someone pressed the reset button. It almost set a new bar. Now I could make plans with someone that didn't just involve me. I didn't want to be without a family or live on the streets anymore. I had a reason to live and her name was Nancy.

I found myself standing in front of someone I actually cared about other than myself. I never thought that would ever be possible. My walls were starting to crack. She was breathtakingly beautiful. I didn't want to take advantage of her. I was afraid if I told her all about my past that she would send me packing. The moment we stepped foot on the dance floor for the first dance—I blushed. It was love at first sight the day I became Nancy's partner.

THE IMPORTANCE OF FATHER FIGURES

The days went by so quickly working for Nacho. I waited to catch a glimpse of her after school. I didn't mind that the days turned into weeks, which turned into months and years working in the grocery store for her father. Nancy made me want to become a better person.

I even quit doing drugs for her.

I'll never forget the day I told her that I loved her. We were holding hands walking over the Williamsburg Bridge. I told her that it was because of my love for her that I had recently become clean. When she told me that she loved me back—I almost fainted. I knew right then that I wanted to spend the rest of my life with her.

I gave up the drugs and alcohol. I wanted to put *all* of the past in my rear view. She gave me the courage to dream. For the first time in my life, I stopped living scared. I was so used to living day-by-day—sometimes hour-by-hour. Now, I was a person who dreamed and thought of the future.

I wasn't going to let anything or anyone stop me— including Nacho. Nacho loved having me as a worker. Someone to be there twenty four-seven to watch over the store. Whether I was working or sleeping, I was always there. He never had to worry about the store.

I never said anything to him about Nancy, but I didn't have to. He saw the looks we gave each other when she came home from school. He never came out and said anything to me, but I could tell that he did *not* like me talking to his daughter. If you think Puerto Rican mothers are protective— the fathers are worse! I knew he had a license to carry and that he owned a gun. There was never a day I saw him without a gun strapped to his waist.

Although I respected Nacho, I loved Nancy even more. Nancy and I saw each other behind Nacho's back. We planned to hang out on the weekends when Nancy and her sisters met their friends. Before reaching their final destination, we always met at Kosciusko Station. Her sisters would get back on the train, but we went our separate ways.

I longed to hold her hand. It didn't matter if we explored New York City or sat on a bench in Central Park for hours. As long as I was with her—nothing else mattered. No matter what we did, we always made sure to meet up with her sisters before going back home. This way Nacho wouldn't find out.

This was around the time I decided to go back to school. Even though I had been thrown out of every school, I wanted to be Nancy's partner for the rest of my life. I needed to graduate. I was desperate.

I didn't want anyone, including her, to find out that I couldn't read. I knew I couldn't stay working for her father for the rest of my life. So I asked around. My cousin was living in an apartment building nearby on Gates and Bushwick that only charged $15 per month for a furnished room. I was making $110 per month working for Nacho so I asked the landlord if I could rent it. My cousin vouched for me, and he let me rent the room from him.

I knew I needed to find a way to support the both of us if I was going to ask her to marry me so I enrolled in Sterling's High School on Pacific Avenue in Brooklyn. The school employed teachers that made six hundred dollars more than other school teachers in the area. Six hundred was code for putting up with juvenile delinquents, Special Ed, and at risk kids. It felt like *every* teacher was six feet and above so they could break up a fight. The fighting was constant. It was a wonder anyone learned anything.

Sterling's had only *one* entrance to the school. They built the school to house the toughest of the tough. The worst students in Brooklyn.

I was one of them.

I spent most of my life getting into trouble. As soon as I came to Sterling's I met their school psychologist named Gus Sosa. Even though my attitude had softened some because of Nancy—I never let anyone else see it but her. But Gus saw right through me too. He made me think. Every day, when he saw me walking down the halls—he would pause and look at me.

Willie you know there's something just for you in this life, right? You can become something, he said.

I wasn't the speechless type, but I didn't know how to answer him. The only response I could muster was something smart-alecky. My mouth was *always* getting me into trouble.

Gus knew this.

I knew this.

But, he taught me how to think of clever solutions in my mind *before* acting them out. I was wild man. He was the first person to ever speak to me in that way! He taught me what self-esteem looked like. My dad *never* told me he loved me or that he was proud of me.

The Sterling's School Principal, Sally Walker, and Gus Sosa both became father figures to me. Sally was the first African American to play for St. John's University Basketball. He was a historic guy in New York. It was a *b-i-g* deal for him to pay attention to me, or even care about me. Every other principal before him either caught me getting into trouble or kicked me out of their school because of the trouble I was causing.

There was no middle ground.

Gus and Sally talked to me in a way that no one had ever spoken to me before. My mind was spinning. I couldn't stop thinking.

Maybe I'm not going to die on the streets. Maybe there was something for me in the future. Maybe I could marry Nancy.

Their words planted thoughts in my mind. Once their thoughts pierced my heart, I knew what Gus said was right. I knew Sally believed in me that I could become something. That I could do something with my life. I didn't have to repeat what happened in my home growing up in Brooklyn. When that switch turned on in my head—I believe what these men were saying about me was true. I just had a hard time connecting the thoughts in my head to believing them in my heart. They gave me the courage to dream for a future.

A future with Nancy.

I told Nancy that I gave up drugs for her. I believed her when she told me she loved me. I didn't say *how long* I gave up drugs for her because I thought love would save me. It only took me six months before I realized there was *one* other voice that was calling me back, and its name was marijuana.

When you were young, did anyone take a chance on you like Nacho, Gus Sosa, or Principal Sally Walker did for me? Perhaps it was a family member, or someone who wasn't part of your family—but someone who believed in you? Please take a few minutes and answer the questions below, before moving on to Chapter 4 in *It's A New Beginning: How to Turn Setbacks Into Comebacks*.

QUESTIONS

1. Did anyone take a chance on you when you were young? If so, who and why?
2. Have you ever experienced love at first sight? Why or why not?
3. Who or what makes you want to become a better person?
4. Who was your father figure growing up? Why?
5. Do you remember how old you were when you believed "you can become something" in this life?

CHAPTER 4: LOVE AND BASKETBALL

I am a confident kid. I'm a Brooklyn boy, *remember?* I honestly don't remember a day that I wasn't true to myself since my mom kicked me out of the house at age eleven. Never once did I question my motives while livin' on the streets. I answered to *n-o-b-o-d-y*, but me.

I didn't have time for daydreams until Nancy entered the picture. For the first time in my life, I wrestled with thoughts of the future. I wasn't sure I had what it takes. To make matters worse—I lied to Nancy about my drug habits. I had to. I believed if I told her that I went back to smoking pot, she would leave me.

I wanted to do right by Nancy. I knew doing drugs behind her back was wrong. But, there was no way I would give up Nancy that easy. She was the best thing that ever happened to me, remember? She gave me a reason, other than myself, to live.

I never fully realized the weight of my drug habit until I tried to quit. It honestly felt like I had a monkey on my back that I couldn't shake off. Pot held me captive. Its voice had a stronghold on my life. The darkness of my past threatened to steal any silver lining of a future with Nancy. My negative thoughts choked up all of the positive feelings I had.

I don't feel worthy. I'm not good enough. I should be dead.

Snap out of it! I told myself. *I'm Willie Alfonso! If I can survive a crushed foot and being in a coma, I could do this! I could be a better man and partner that Nancy deserved.*

Her parents were another story though. Night after night, the silence echoed as I laid in bed awake trying to figure out a plan. I was used to going from Plan A to Plan Z on a dime, remember?

Should I tell Nancy about my drug habit or should I not? Should I risk asking Nacho for permission to marry his daughter or not?

I choose to ask. I remember opening the door to their upstairs apartment.

Here goes nothing, I told myself.

When I opened the door, I saw Nancy's eyes light up. Her mother, Ĩrma, was doing dishes. She shot me a look that wasn't exactly welcoming. I could tell she wasn't exactly pleased to see me upstairs in their apartment. When Nacho came out into the living room I swallowed real hard, and asked him for permission to date Nancy. I knew I wanted to ask for permission to marry her, but I couldn't stomach the words. I thought by asking for permission to date their daughter—they might say *yes*.

Wait here, he said.

Where was Nacho going? I thought.

My lungs gasped for air. I didn't have time to breath because Ĩrma started tearing down the drapes in a fit of rage.

Nancy didn't speak.

I didn't speak.

We both sat there too scared to move.

Two whole hours went by before Nacho reappeared. Two hours. I didn't need to look up because I could smell the alcohol on his breath the minute Nacho opened the upstairs door. He was drunk. Nacho took one look at me and pointed his gun in my face.

I ran.

I was used to running, remember? My courage had quickly melted into fear. I thought her mom trusted me? Why had my heart been awakened only to be shot to hell by her dad?

Unfortunately, I didn't have a plan for what just happened. I was making just enough to survive. I was used to surviving though. Every day I hustled—before it became a hit song.

I had this feeling like I would never rise above, and Nacho's actions proved my thoughts right. But, when Gus Sosa entered the picture—he showed me respect. Something I had never received from any man before. Gus didn't let me get away with smart-mouthing him or anyone else for that matter. Because he took the time to listen to me, he looked deeper than any man had before. I was terrified that he'd see through my thug exterior. Instead of exploiting my façade, he told me that I could be somebody with my life, remember? He was the first to give me permission to rise above my circumstances.

If it weren't for Gus and Sally, I don't think I would have made it through that rough transition of needing to find a new job. Both Gus and Sally were like father figures to me, but it was Principal Walker who put his words into action. He bent over backwards with the school board, and asked me to work with him at Youth Services Agency (YSA) coaching basketball in Manhattan.

There were two things and *only* two things in life I loved: Nancy and basketball. Sure, Nancy softened my heart, but in my head—I was still looking for my ticket out of the ghetto.

When Nacho took a chance on me, I had no idea I would fall in love with his daughter. When Sally Walker hired me, I had no idea I would be counseling kids to get off drugs and to stay in school.

I was barely hanging on myself, and so far no one knew that I couldn't read. I already felt like a traitor, but Sally was a New York celebrity, remember? How could I say *no* to Principal Walker? Right after Principal Walker hired me, he told me to meet him at Sterling's Park, which was the same park I used to smoke pot.

I froze.

Did he know?

It was all I could do to contain my composure and look him straight in the eyes.

I wasn't only lying to Nancy. I was also keeping the truth from Gus Sosa and Principal Walker. I'm not the type of person to hide my emotions. If you want to know how I'm doing—*just ask*. I'm not afraid to tell it like it is either.

I'm Puerto Rican. That's what we do!

My conscience hated lying to Nancy, Gus, and Sally, which also happened to be the three people I cared most about. Every time I entered through Sterling's High one big door, I had to be very careful. I didn't want any of the students or teachers to smell pot on my clothes in case they ratted me out to Gus or Principal Walker.

Marijuana wasn't exactly the easiest scent to hide. Plus, I didn't have many clothes to wear. Even though I had my own apartment, I was only working for YSA since the day Nacho pointed a gun in my face and I fled from his apartment. Now, I was about to find out how it felt to lie to the youth as well.

LIVING A DOUBLE LIFE

How was I supposed to tell these kids to say *no* to drugs? I wasn't. I hadn't been able to stop smoking pot and drinking for more than six months at a time. Six months! I wanted to stop, but smoking pot was all I knew. It brought me comfort until it didn't.

I felt like a hypocrite teaching the kids something I couldn't teach myself. I started questioning *why* Principal Walker hired me in the first place. My not-so-recent past of livin' on the streets and eating out of garbage cans would, at the very least, help me to earn the kids trust. And it did. These kids were looking for excuses to push adults away, but I didn't scare easily. Plus I wasn't quite an adult yet. The kids in street gangs were the first to show me respect.

His name was Francisco. He was also Puerto Rican and was from the Lower East Side on 4th Street. He loved basketball—and he was good at it too. If I could run as fast as lightning, this kid could shoot a three pointer with his eyes closed.

Hakim was an African American from a street gangs on 4th street. He was the Wilt Chamberlain, or center of the group.

Basketball was just as good for the kids as it was for me. It was a unifying sport. No matter the color of your skin, what 'hood you grew up, or street gang you associated with— *all* the kids loved the interaction. Basketball was a great way to burn off steam and create healthy competition. I think that's why the youth liked me. I got into it with them.

Basketball was my life.

I could be coaching a pickup game or two, and the hours would fly by without realizing it was time to go, or that I was no longer getting paid. Maybe that's why Principal Walker hired me. I always looked forward to the afternoons when I got to spend time with the youth after school.

Nobody knew I was living a double life.

Life was pretty great. I had my own place and the two loves of my life. I couldn't wait to meet up with Nancy for date night. We met at our spot, the Metropolitan Avenue Station near Bushwick High School. I had to see her, hold her hand, and kiss her cheek.

She was my girl. I loved her so much. Nancy *never* let me touch her. She respected herself. She was the classiest lady I knew. In fact, Nancy was the definition of class. It's just one of the many reasons why I fell more in love with her with each passing day. Nancy made me want to be a better person, remember?

When we arrived at the station, we sat down and I put my arms around her. How did I miss the tears in her eyes? When I tried to wipe them off her cheek, she startled.

Who hurt you? I asked.

I couldn't help my anger. I wanted to punch whomever hurt her in the face right in that moment.

Nacho, she said.

That was all she had to say. Right then, I knew our cover was blown.

Who told? I asked.

It was only a matter of time before her parents found out we were dating. The relationship Nacho had already forbidden. Nancy laid her head back on my shoulder and cried. She must have cried for an hour. I loved Nancy with all my heart. Each tear she cried felt like my heart was shattering into a million pieces. When she calmed down, she told me the whole story.

As luck would have it, one of her friends from Bushwick High School spotted us making out at the train station. We were always so careful to meet up with her sisters on the weekends at Kosciusko Station or the Metropolitan Station during the week. I thought all of Nancy's friends knew not to tell her parents.

Maybe it was one of the friends who spotted me waiting for her to get out of school. Or maybe one of her friends spotted us making out at the train station. Whoever it was rated us out! It wasn't like we were the *only* couple making out, but that wasn't the scary part.

I didn't want to lose Nancy, but I didn't want to make her choose between her dad and me. I knew how it felt to be on the receiving end of that choice. I was so afraid Nancy was going to choose her father over me.

What was so wrong with me that all the men in my life felt the need to make the women in my life choose?

We both sat in silence for what felt like hours. At least I had a place to stay and a job working for Principal Walker. But Nancy? Nobody could replace Nancy.

I knew Nancy could see through my tough exterior, as always, but I was *not* going to cry in front of her. I couldn't. I was too stunned to react. Every painful memory from my past came flooding back to my mind. All my walls threatened to break against the damn I had built for myself as a safety precaution. And now? It was threatening to burst.

I knew what was at stake.

It frustrated me that the *only* family that accepted me, trusted me, and gave me a job was now disowning me too.

Why couldn't I be someone's first choice? Maybe there was something wrong with me? Was it because I was a dark skinned Puerto Rican, and Nancy's family was light skinned?

I experienced a *lot* of racism growing up Brooklyn. I felt it every day in the streets, at school, and now her family. I was an *outcast* according to Nacho. Thankfully, Nancy didn't feel that way.

When it was time for her to go home, we hugged goodbye. Nancy cried again. I felt so helpless. I wasn't sure if I was ever going to see her again. How in the world were we going to make our relationship work?

Once again, It seemed as if fate was against me. Against us. I didn't get any sleep that night. I went home and laid on my bed trying to think of a plan. I was good at thinking of plans, but no plans came to my mind. Wave after wave, feelings of depression hit me as I tossed and turned in my bed for what felt like an eternity.

Did anyone ever threaten to stand between you and someone you cared about? Maybe it wasn't a romantic relationship or love interest—but a close friend or family member? Maybe it was because of the color of your skin, your 'hood, education—or lack of education. Please take a few minutes and answer the questions below, before moving on to Chapter 5 in *It's A New Beginning: How to Turn Setbacks Into Comebacks.*

QUESTIONS

1. Have you ever lived a double life or felt like a hypocrite? Why?
2. What's your favorite sport to watch? To play? Why?
3. What do you think is worse: loving someone deeply and losing them, or never loving at all?

CHAPTER 5: GOING TO THE CHAPEL

Nancy was completing her last year at Bushwick High School, but I still had one more year to go at Sterling's High School. If I wanted to marry her, I needed to make more money so that I could support us. In order to make more money, I needed a better paying job. And, in order to find a better paying job, I needed to be able to work full time, which meant I needed to drop out of school. Again.

I didn't have the heart to tell Principal Walker or Gus Sosa to their faces. I knew they would try to talk me out of quitting so I knew when the time came—I would just quit showing up at school and YSA altogether. It broke my heart. They believed in me and I didn't want to let them down, but I felt I didn't have any choice.

I couldn't wait to meet up with Nancy and tell her all of *my* plans for us. I hoped she wouldn't talk me out of them as well. When we met at the station—I shared my plans to get a better job and find a bigger apartment. I told her I was all in. I left nothing back.

When she agreed, I was kind of caught off guard. I didn't question her even though I was pleasantly surprised. She had basically agreed to marry me and let me drop out of school! I was beyond grateful that Nancy would *choose* me. Maybe there wasn't anything wrong with me after all. For the first time in my life, someone chose me, Willie!

I knew she was used to living well, her family was off. Their family's apartment above the grocery store was nice. I didn't have much, but I immediately put myself in the provider role. I knew I wanted to be the man of her dreams and take care of her because she was such a lady!

Oh man, was she!

Before I could go looking for an apartment that I probably couldn't afford—I was about to be in for a surprise. If I thought Nancy's agreeing to marry me was huge—just wait! My luck was about to change. Before I could get to work on *our* plans—I heard from William Floyd PS 59 that I had won a settlement.

Remember when my left foot was crushed in a construction accident? I had completely forgotten that my case ever went to court because it had been over ten years. When they contacted me I couldn't believe it. I never thought the case would make it to trial, or that I would get a settlement. Almost a decade went by with no word. It just so happened that the time I needed help the most—I actually got it. That *n-e-v-e-r* happened to me!

I hopped on the train right away to pick up my check at a Law Firm on Broadway in Manhattan. By law, the lady wasn't allowed to tell me the amount over the phone. I couldn't get a hold of Nancy because her parents had already forbidden our relationship. I would have to wait until our date in the evening to tell her the good news.

I got there as soon as I could. A lady in a navy suit handed me an envelope. I didn't want to seem too eager.

Thank You, I said.

I quickly walked back outside. I walked all the way to the subway entrance. I didn't open the envelope until I was back on the train. I thought I won a few hundred bucks at most. Nope! When I looked down into the crisp white envelope the amount was staggering.

Two thousand and five hundred dollars. I couldn't make this stuff up if I tried man. Twenty five hundred dollars dollars was a *b-i-g* deal in 1972. I couldn't wait to tell Nancy in person that we could finally get married.

The look on her face that night was priceless. She was so beautiful. I threw my arms around her to hug her. Nancy cried tears of joy. I cried a little too—I'm not going to lie.

Nancy and I were getting married. I couldn't wait to marry my sweetheart and the love of my life—the best thing that ever happened to me.

The next day, I began searching for an apartment. I found a two bedroom apartment on 310 Central Avenue in Brooklyn for $320 a month. I was even able to pay to furnish the entire apartment. Nancy and I devised a plan to get all of her belongings over to the new apartment without anyone finding out. She would drop off her clothes at the dry cleaners, and give me the receipt so I could pick them up when they were ready. We did this for a few weeks before the house was fully furnished.

We both knew that when we got married we couldn't tell anyone—including her sisters. The night she usually went out with her sisters, instead of meeting up at Kosciusko Station, we decided to elope. I asked my friend Eddy if he would be our witness. The tough part was reconnecting with my mom. Nancy was eighteen and I was seventeen, and I needed my mom's signature to get married.

I was relieved when she showed up to sign our marriage license, which only cost us twenty five dollars. The pastor down the street from the new apartment agreed to marry us. I don't remember the name of the Pentecostal Church, but I remember it was off Central and Greene.

FAMILY DRAMA

When Nancy didn't come home with her sisters that night, we knew her parents would worry. I asked my friend Eddy to meet up with Nancy's sisters outside La Mancha club where they would be dancing. He waited around until the club closed to tell them we were not meeting them at the train statin. Then, he told them the news.

Nancy and I had eloped.

We knew we couldn't risk telling her parents in person because of what happened last time—so we sent Eddy to be our messenger instead.

Nancy took being separated from her family pretty hard because we got married. I was already used to being disowned, but not my Sweetheart Nancy.

Almost immediately after we got married, my mom became fixated on destroying our marriage. It was as if inviting my mom to the wedding gave her permission to come back into my life. This is what I was worried about. She practiced a blend of Catholicism and African Voodoo called Santeria. Both of my parents practiced it, actually. Their religion was actually quite popular among the French and Spanish colonies who, during the Atlantic slave trade, adopted the Voodoo practices of the Africans. The mixture became known as Santeria. You could tell if someone was practicing because they wore different color beads—each representing a different god.

It was an easy decision to distance ourselves from Nancy's family after we eloped, but my mom was a different story. She accused Nancy of keeping me from a relationship with her. On the contrary, it was Nancy who always pushed me to have a relationship with my mom in spite of all the hell she put me through with my dad. In fact, it wasn't until I started writing out my story in this book that I remembered.

My mom abused me too.

When you experience child abuse at a young age, sometimes you forget, or block out the painful memories. It's been hard to have *a-l-l* those memories come back like a flood.

For instance, the issue I had with my mother actually started before the issues with my father. Before he pushed her out of a window. Before he disowned me and made me live on the streets and eat out of garbage cans.

I remember one of my cousins came to live with us in Brooklyn for a short time. It was during this time that someone set a fire to my mom's closet. It wasn't me. My mom accused me of starting the fire, and punished me by lighting my hand on fire. I still have a scar on my left hand on my middle finger from her burning me with matches.

There were other things she used to make me do like kneel on rice until the rice literally embedded itself into my skin. I knew I remembered that story for a reason, but I thought it was because my friends parents forced them to kneel. Nope! My mom did that to me too.

Then there was the time she beat my brothers and sisters and I with the shower hose. We lived in what's called a railroad apartment. You could literally walk straight through our apartment starting with the kitchen and ending with the living room. The bathtub was in the kitchen with a shower curtain around it, and we used a rubber hose for the shower head. When my mom was angry with us, she used to beat the crap out of us with that thing man.

Moving forward, this was the kind of family drama I was trying to *a-v-o-i-d*. And yet—my Sweetheart Nancy—knew how important family was. She encouraged me every time I wanted to give up on my mother. She knew it was important to have a relationship with her. I did forgive my mom, but that doesn't mean we have a close relationship.

HUSBAND *AND* FATHER

While we were living like a married couple, I struggled on and off with doing drugs and getting clean. The honeymoon phase was a powerful deterrent to doing drugs. After a while, the addiction came back. I desperately wanted love to save me. It didn't. I thought the family drama was behind us now. It wasn't. I should have known better.

I heard from my brothers that our dad fathered *many* other kids from all over the world because he was a merchant seaman. He was not only a coward, but he was a cheater in my book. I wanted nothing to do with him so I stayed away from all the drama. I had no interest in connecting with or meeting any of my half siblings. Besides, I was too busy trying to figure out this thing called being a husband.

I was clueless. I had absolutely no point of reference on what it meant to be a husband to Nancy. No mentor to ask when life got hard or if I just had any questions about marriage. My parents were never there for me. Their marriage was the exact opposite of what I wanted.

Nancy was a sweetheart. My sweetheart. She was a gentle woman who, unfortunately, married a gangster. I couldn't help myself. Everything was a fight. I didn't know how to be Nancy's husband. I was shocked out of my mind that she said *yes* when I asked her to marry me. There were many days I pestered her with my questions. I needed reassurance.

How could you love this? I asked.

Each time she'd have the same response. She'd just look at me with those big brown eyes and give me that *one* look. I knew that look very well. I don't know why, but I always responded negatively.

How in the world could you love me? I'm a piece of crap. I'm undereducated. I can't read. I can't write. I'm dark skinned.

Nancy was the first person that loved me, and I couldn't deal with it. My father or mother never once said *I love you*. Now, I had this woman telling me she loved me. Marriage was amazing but it certainly wasn't easy. It was the best thing that happened to me, and the scariest.

Sometimes, I would smoke pot to take the edge off my fears. To find a sense of calm. As much as it killed me to admit my own inadequacies, I felt exposed. I wanted so badly to get clean, but no matter how hard I tried—it actually made things worse. So much worse, in fact, that I turned to harder drugs like I had done in the past with acid. Only this time, I started doing cocaine. It was a very, very bad drug to do when you're a husband and about to be a father.

After two years of marriage, Nancy gave birth to a beautiful baby girl we named Venus. If marriage scared me, being a father scared the living daylights out of me. I didn't know how to be a husband *and* a father.

Every day I struggled to accept and receive their love and grace. I was clueless man. The *only* thing I knew how to do was work, work, and more work. I wasn't afraid of work because it was the one thing I could control.

After Venus was born, I found a better paying job working for Lou Harris & Associates in Manhattan. I learned how to run his small printing machine for the pollsters. Just because I couldn't read and write didn't mean I was stupid. I wasn't. I made over $300 per week. Back then that was really good money.

A few years after Venus was born, we welcomed a second daughter named Yvette into the world. I put in for more hours at work, and they let me work as much overtime as I wanted.

Honestly, my idea of being a good husband and father meant providing for my family. I thought not being violent or abusive—something my father *couldn't* do—should earn me Husband and Father of the Year Award. It didn't. I wasn't even close to learning what it meant to be there for my wife and my daughters. All the time I spent away from home working put a strain on my marriage, and my relationship with Venus and Yvette.

I was scared to be home. Scared to let them see me scared. Scared I'd get caught doing drugs.

MY NUMBER ONE FEAR

My drug habit was spiraling out of control. I didn't know how to stop it. I was afraid. I could no longer stop the what ifs from coming.

What if I bought a bad bag of cocaine? That's honestly how I thought my life was going to end.

What if Nancy left me and took the girls with her? The thought of living without them terrorized me.

What if I overdosed? Who would provide for my girls after I was dead? I thought this every time I got high or shot up.

I was tempted to believe they were better off without me. Just when I thought I couldn't hang in there any longer, I got a new job at Oppenheimer & Company.

My supervisor's name was Otto Lang. I didn't know it yet, but he was about to make an impact on my life so big it would change the entire course of my life and my family.

I know I'm not the only one with family drama. Every family has its troubles whether through blood or their in-laws. Please take a few minutes and answer the questions below, before moving on to Chapter 6 in *It's A New Beginning: How to Turn Setbacks Into Comebacks.*

QUESTIONS
1. What was the best thing that ever happened to you?
2. What makes you feel inadequate?
3. Have you ever been welcomed into a new family or been kicked out of one because of something you said or did?
4. What is your number one fear and why?

CHAPTER 6: THE DAY I MET OTTO LANG

Work became my middle name. It had to, in order to provide for my family. As my responsibilities at home were increasing, so did my insecurities. Although my job at Oppenheimer & Company was going well, I did what any good family man would do—*work*.

I threw myself into more hours at work. I learned how to manage an even larger printing press. It was much bigger than the one at Lou Harris & Associates. It was at my new job that I perfected my hustling ways. Even though I *still* couldn't read or write, I was always super careful when the guys at the shop approached me with a problem. I'd take a good, hard look at the paper—pretending I could read it—then look at them like I knew what I was talking about.

What do you think we should do? I asked.

No matter what problem I came up against at work or at home, I always found a way around it. I was getting pretty good at living a double life. My coworkers didn't know that I couldn't read. As the company continued to grow, they hired a new supervisor.

His name was Otto Lang.

He immediately stood out. There were about sixty guys in the shop, all Hispanic or African American. Otto was German. He had blonde hair and blue eyes.

Man, we're gonna eat this boy up! I thought.

That's when he said it. The one thing I did not expect to come out of his mouth.

Willie, I just want to tell you something brother. Jesus loves you. I jerked my hand out of his hand shake and yelled at him.

Where was your Jesus when I was eating out of garbage cans? Where was your Jesus when I was livin' in that abandoned building, and got woken up by rats biting my feet? Where was your Jesus when my father threw my mother out of that window? I don't need that Jesus stuff man. That's for white people not for me. Keep that Jesus crap to yourself.

His statement infuriated me so bad that I had to stop and catch my breath. Otto just smiled.

Jesus loves you, he said again calmly.

I thought Otto was mental. I found it so odd that he tried to convince *all* the guys in the shop that we were going to have a Bible study. He would open up his Bible, read a verse to us, and then explain what it meant. Then, he'd tell everyone in the room that Jesus loved them. The next day, he'd do the same thing all over again. And the next day, and the next. Bible. Verse. Explanation.

Jesus loves you, he would say.

I got so annoyed that I started showing up to work a few minutes early so I could glue his Bible shut. The glue at the print shop wasn't your run of the mill glue. They had the *best* glue. The kind that was like super glue. I made sure to put tons of this magic glue all around his Bible so he couldn't open it anymore.

Otto outsmarted me.

He walked his Bible right over to the cutters and cut the glue off his Bible. It worked. Nothing deterred this guy. I actually glued his Bible shut three, maybe four times until I realized I couldn't stop this brother from hosting Bible studies at work.

There was something different about Otto Lang that scared me a little bit. And I wasn't afraid of anything or anyone. So I tried another tactic. Two minutes before the Bible Study, I went into the room and lit up two or three joints to smoke the place up.

I figured, if we all had to sit there and listen to Otto talk about Jesus and read the Bible—at least *he* was going to get a contact high.

It didn't work.

Otto opened his Bible, read a verse, gave us an explanation and said those famous three words again.

THE REAL DEAL

The thing with Otto is that he was for *real*. He was the real deal. A *what-you-see-is-what-you-get* kind of person. At work, he had a jar on his desk that he used to collect money. Every day, he would skip lunch and put the money in the jar to raise money for his son, Carl, who was attending medical school in Guyana.

His goal was to bring Carl home for Christmas. I can't tell you how intimidating that was to me. I had never seen a father love his son so much that he would sacrifice lunch to bring his son home. Every day, his sacrifice continued to intimidate me until one of the guys in the shop decided to steal Otto's lunch money.

That was the wrong decision.

Because Otto was my first introduction to a father loving his son, I wasn't going to let just *anyone* take that away from him, including my co-workers. The very next day, I told the guys in the shop that *if* they stole from Otto they would have a bigger problem—*me*.

Nobody ever stole from Otto Lang again.

Otto was able to afford to bring Carl home for Christmas. Unfortunately, I owed a *lot* of money to drug dealers all over Brooklyn. I had to move my family to Staten Island so they wouldn't find me. I struggled to provide for the family because of my drug habit.

All I could think about was the fact that Otto had sacrificed so much to bring his son home. I was ashamed that I had spent so much of my hard earned money on drugs that could have been spent on more presents for my wife and my kids.

On Christmas Day, I heard a knock on the door. When I looked through the peep hole I saw him.

It's that crazy white dude. Tell him to go away, I told Nancy. She just looked at me like I was the crazy one.

I know you're in there, Otto said.

I waited a few minutes before opening the door. I couldn't believe my eyes. Standing on my door step in Staten Island was Otto, his wife Delores, *and* his son Carl with presents for my family.

I was blown away.

I couldn't deal with Otto Lang and his kindness. No one—and I mean no one—had ever shown me love in that way before. It was foreign to me. Growing up, I thought white people were the enemy. I really struggled to accept this man's generosity.

Two more Christmas' came and went, and Otto got a new job working for Morgan Stanley. Part of me was a little sad when he left, but the other part of me was relieved. It was unnerving working with a guy who was always happy, who had his life together, and knew how to be there for his family. I didn't. No matter how hard I tried—I couldn't get this monkey off my back.

Another few years went by and my drug habit was tearing up my family. I struggled just to show up to work every day because of all the cocaine I was doing.

My whole life was falling apart.

My number one fear was coming true. My wife was threatening to leave me because I couldn't afford to pay the rent anymore. Nancy told me if I continued to do drugs that she'd leave me and take the girls.

She was not joking.

Looking back on that time of my life, I was certain I was going to lose her. The thought of losing the only family that I cared about, and the only people who ever loved me drove me to my breaking point.

BREAKING POINT

I remember that night like it was yesterday. It was a Saturday evening, and I had a bag of cocaine. Before I could get high—I heard a voice.

If you continue doing this you're going to die, it said.

I felt that voice might be God, but I wasn't sure. I didn't believe in God, remember? The only person I knew to ask was Otto Lang. I remember that he had given me his number before he left, but that was two years ago. Would he still be at that number? Would he even remember me?

Hello. I said.

Willie Alfonso, he said.

I didn't even have to say my name! Otto told me he had been waiting for my phone call. I told him everything.

In a matter of minutes, I spilled my guts. I told him about the drugs, that I thought I heard a voice, and that Nancy was leaving me and taking the girls. Before I could finish Otto interrupted me.

My wife, my son, and I have been praying for you and your family Willie. If you think God is telling you something, then it must be Him. But to be sure, why don't you come to church with me tomorrow?

Okay. I'll be there, I said.

I believed him.

He told me he lived in Staten Island also, and gave me the address of his church. Since I couldn't write, I had to remember the address by memory. When I hung up the phone, I told Nancy that I wanted to go to church on Sunday.

She laughed.

Those must be some good drugs you're smoking, she said.

I wasn't going to be dissuaded. I told Nancy that I had just spoken to Otto Lang, and that we were going to church. No if's, and's, or but's about it.

You? Church? She said. *Man you must be high. They're good people—but—you? Church?*

I knew how much Nancy *loved* Otto Lang. I knew she never forgot his kindness that one Christmas when he brought all of us presents.

If you're going to leave me, fine. But, let's just go to church first, I said.

We went to church, but we got lost on the way there. I couldn't remember the exact address. Of course, we had the *b-i-g-g-e-s-t* fight in our married life trying to find the church.

We pulled up late. There in the parking lot were Otto *and* Carl on their knees praying for God to guide us there. We got out of the car and walked into the church. Otto told us we couldn't take the girls in the service with us. We had to put them in Sunday School. I was *not* comfortable giving up our kids to people we didn't know, but I did what I was told.

When the service started, the pastor started preaching everything about my life. I was ticked off, I thought Otto told his pastor about me. Otto and I had it out in the parking lot. He told me that he didn't say anything to the pastor. He said God was speaking to me, but I was too angry to listen.

Once I was back home, I had a few hours to calm down. I was hot man. I knew Nancy was leaving me, but I didn't want to give up that easily. I decided to give it one last shot. I told Nancy that we should go back to the evening service. She told me she didn't want to go.

I went to church by myself.

When the evening service started, the speaker started telling all about my life again. But this was a different guy. Otto wasn't there. This time, I knew it wasn't Otto.

God was speaking to me.

I felt convicted. My heart was beating out of my chest. I didn't want to believe in God, but I felt something drawing me up out of my seat during the altar call.

Before my legs could respond, I had it out with God.

First of all, God, I don't believe You are real. I got nothing to lose here. If I walk down this aisle and give my life to you—you're going to have to get this monkey of drugs off my back. If you're able to do that—nobody on this earth will ever serve you more loyally than I will. Please God. I don't want to lose this woman that I love, and my two children. I will serve you. Just get this monkey off my back.

That's when I felt it. This crazy peace I had never felt before. Like everything was going to work out, and I didn't have it all figured out. Even though I had a million questions racing in my mind, I pushed them aside and walked to the front of the church.

There was Otto's son Carl welcoming me once again.

Jesus loves you, he said just like his dad.

Jesus loves you too brother, I said while choking back the tears.

JESUS LOVES *ME*

Palm Sunday 1981 was the *best* night of my life. I knew only Jesus had the cure to get the monkey of drugs off my back and restore my family. Jesus did in fact love *me*.

Looking back, that's probably why Otto scared me in the first place. It was the Jesus in Otto that scared me the most. I must have known all along Jesus had the power to change my life, but I wasn't ready to listen. Now came the tough part.

How was I going to tell Nancy?

I was scared she wouldn't believe me. My palms were sweaty. My heart was racing even faster than it did during the altar call when the pastor asked people to come forward. I felt like I was having a panic attack when I told Nancy that I asked Jesus into my heart.

She wasn't convinced.

I know you're lying to me, she said.

I'm dead serious, I said.

I did my best to convince her to come with me to the mid-week service. For the first time in my life, I was fighting to save my marriage and my children.

She finally agreed to come with me, and we went together. Three days after I became a Christian, Nancy gave her life to the Lord. On that Wednesday night, everything changed.

It was a new beginning.

Our new beginning.

I remember hugging Nancy with tears in my eyes when one of the pastors came over to pray with us. I couldn't believe it!

We were starting our new beginning with God together. Little did we know that God had many more surprises waiting for us—our first of many comebacks.

The night I walked to the front of the church to give my heart to Christ, everything changed. Life is full of setbacks or breaking points, but it's also full of comebacks. Before I get to the part on breakthrough—please take a few minutes and answer the questions below, before moving on to Chapter 7 in *It's A New Beginning: How to Turn Setbacks Into Comebacks.*

QUESTIONS

1. Have you ever met anyone who was the *real* deal? How did you know they were who they said they were? Why?
2. Have you experienced a breaking point? If so, who did you turn to? Why?
3. Have you ever come to a point in your life where you can say with confidence that Jesus loves *me*? Who was the first person you told, and how did they respond?

CHAPTER 7: THE DAY I FORGAVE MY FATHER

After we became Christians, our church encouraged us to get more involved. One of their pastors, Pastor Frank Sarcone, asked us if we wanted to get baptized. We said yes, but before we agreed to go through with it—I asked what was required.

Pastor Frank told us we needed to take a class called *Growing in Christ* on Wednesdays nights. I remember peeking through the window like it was yesterday. I saw the teacher reading from a book while asking others to read different passages out loud.

It freaked me out man.

Nobody besides my family knew I couldn't read. *N-o-b-o-d-y*. I was tempted to blow him off, but something told me I could trust this brother.

Can I be honest with you? I asked. *I can't read. There is no way I am going to be humiliated in front of the class.*

Pastor Frank, who quickly became one of my dearest friends and first-ever Bible teachers, looked at me. He gave me the same stupid smile Otto Lang gave me the day I met him.

God will make a way. I'll get back to you, he said.

A couple of weeks later, Frank called me at home and said there was a lady in the church named Angelica Valentin who was willing to teach me how to read. He asked if I wanted to meet Angelica and her husband, John, after the Sunday service.

I agreed.

When I met Angelica and John—I couldn't believe it. They were Puerto Rican like Nancy and I. While our church was over 95% white, the Valentine's definitely made me feel comfortable through the whole process. I went over to their house every Tuesday and Thursday for tutoring.

Angelica gave me the book *See Sally Run*, the same book I read as a kid in William Floyd PS 59 Elementary School.

I was humiliated.

I told her I read that book in first grade. I didn't want to read it again. Thankfully, Angelica didn't take *no* for an answer. She called me on my frustration and set me straight right away.

Willie you have to look at it this way. It's like there's this giant tree in front of you, and you're holding a little ax. Learning how to read isn't going to happen in a day, in a week, or even in a month. It may take a year or two. But you have to start somewhere.

I was this twenty-seven year old kid who was a slow learner. Sure enough, though, Angelica was right. After two years of going over to her house for tutoring, I learned how to read. The entire time, she was *very* Christian with me. I felt like such a gangster, but I knew God was still working with me.

Angelica gave me the tools. She invested in my future. Nobody had ever done that before. It was during those couple of years that I developed an amazing friendship with Angelica and her husband John. I didn't realize *how* much I missed having a father figure in my life until we met. It had been years since Gus Sosa and Sally Walker took me under their wings.

John and Angelica opened up their home, taught me how to read, and helped me to become a better husband and father. I felt so much more confident knowing I finally had someone to go to whenever I needed advice. Little did I know just how much I would need their wisdom and guidance in the coming years.

Getting baptized and learning how to read was the first of many comebacks. I made it a point to reconcile with Nancy's parents after we became Christians. I asked Nacho and Irma to forgive me for eloping with their daughter. I told Nacho that I had *no right* to violate his authority over his daughter that way.

He forgave me.

It was a powerful moment man. Nacho was ill, and he made me promise that I would send Nancy to college after Venus and Yvette were old enough. He had always wanted Nancy to finish her education.

I made him that promise.

Restoring my relationship with Nancy's parents was the right thing to do. Besides my Uncle Frank, Nacho was the only person to let me sleep in his apartment. Although it was in the basement, I wasn't homeless or living on the streets anymore. Because of Nacho, I met my wife. I'm grateful Nacho and I became friends before it was too late.

I visited Nacho in the hospital when his health had taken a turn for the worse. I felt compelled to tell him about Jesus. I couldn't help but share just how much Jesus changed my life, and how I had become a better husband to Nancy and father to the girls because of my relationship with Christ.

I was honored to have Nacho pray with me. He accepted Jesus into his heart before he passed away. After the funeral, Nancy's mom, Ĩrma, came to live with us. She lived with us for a few years. It was during that time we spoke to her about Jesus. She said that if God was real that He would find her a place to live—on her own.

Ĩrma had married young. She had seven kids. She had never lived on her own before. God answered her prayers in a big way when a subsidized condominium opened up. This was such an answer to prayer. It filled Ĩrma with so much hope to believe in God. To this day, she still lives in the same condo and is a follower of Christ.

SURPRISED BY GOD

God did so much in our family after we became Christians. God redeemed my past setbacks one by one, and gave me hope for future comebacks.

Isaiah 43:1 says, "But now, this is what the Lord says—he who created you, Jacob, he who formed you, Israel: 'Do not fear, for I have redeemed you; I have summoned you by name; you are mine.'"

Many years after Nancy and I made the most important decision of our lives—things were going well. Until they weren't. We were surprised when Nancy got sick. Really sick. I was still learning how to trust God with my family. Nancy was my Sweetheart and the mother to my two children, Venus and Yvette.

Why couldn't God test me in another area? Why couldn't I be the sick one?

Nancy was my world. My mind raced through all the negative what ifs.

What if Nancy had something serious? What if she needed surgery?

I was used to going from Plan A to Plan B to Plan Z on a dime, remember? For the first time in my life, instead of figuring things out myself—I got down on my knees. I prayed and begged God to heal her.

I told Nancy she should go to the doctor. Nancy wasn't the kind of person that liked people fussing over here. When she finally arranged to go to the doctors, I went with her.

The doctor performed a few tests to see what was going on. When he came back into the room, I braced myself for the worst. Before I could have words with God, the doctor broke the silence with a smile.

You're pregnant Mrs. Alfonso, he said.

She's what, I said?

My jaw dropped. Nancy looked at me in disbelief. I was speechless. Nancy jokes that I can talk for her and a few other people. I had no words. I don't think I said more than five words on the way back from the doctors. Our girls were already seventeen and fifteen. The pregnancy definitely came as a surprise. We were definitely not expecting God to surprise us with a tiny miracle.

After we recovered from the shock, I saw this as God giving us a new beginning. Another comeback. He was giving me a second chance to be the husband and father He always knew I could be. I knew this was a test of trust. I was learning how to put God first, my family second, and me third.

Proverbs 3:5-6 says, "Trust in the Lord with all your heart and lean not on your own understanding; in all your ways submit to Him, and He will make your paths straight."

Trust was *very* difficult to learn. I had to transfer my own understanding. I had to transfer trusting in what *I* could do. I trusted in *me*. It took me many years to learn how to come to the Lord with all my stuff. I was so sick and tired of preachers preaching that everything's going to be alright once you become a Christian. That's a straight up lie! Everything is not going to be okay. However, I'd rather go through life with God than trusting solely in myself.

Nine months later, Nancy and I welcomed our third baby girl named Krista into our lives, making our family of five complete.

I had a rule with my daughters, Venus and Yvette, before Krista was born. Whenever they wanted to go on a date with a guy, he had to come over to the house to ask for my permission. Man to man. I would then walk him into my room and show him a little box.

Can you read the writing on the inside of the box, I'd ask?

No, he'd say.

This was a test. Of course he couldn't because the box was shut. Inside that little box was one thousand dollars. I told him it was *bail money*. If he tried or did anything to hurt my daughter—I intended on using that money to bail myself out of jail! When Krista was born, I joked with the girls that I needed to keep the money even longer!

DOING GOD'S WORK

I came into this world with luggage. I got my family back *because* I learned how to transfer my trust to God. He taught me how to be there for my family. How to reconcile with Nancy's family. How to be the best husband and father I could be to Venus, Yvette, and Krista. Thanks be to God, He even helped get rid of the monkey of drugs off my back once and for all. I had to learn how to acknowledge God.

Matthew 6:33 says, "But seek first his kingdom and his righteousness, and all these things will be given to you as well."

I acknowledged that I made a lot of mistakes as a husband and father. I hurt my wife and my kids. I caused strife in the home. If I had to do it all over again, I'd be a better listener. It was a journey. Trust was a s-l-o-w process. The more luggage I had—the more it took to learn how to renew my mind while trusting in God.

Romans 12:2 says, "Do not conform to the pattern of this world, but be transformed by the renewing of your mind. Then you will be able to test and approve what God's will is—his good, pleasing and perfect will."

Once God renewed my mind, God changed my heart. Everything I believed about God was coming true, but my heart needed to catch up. I knew God was calling me to ministry, but it wasn't until after Nancy and I taught Sunday School that I knew God had work for me to do. She taught and I did all the demonstrations. We enjoyed leading Sunday School together so much that we switched to Middle School, and then to High School many years later as our youngest daughter, Krista, got older.

I loved that our church was very missionary minded. We hosted missionaries in our home often. I thought God was calling me to be a missionary so I jumped at the chance to go on a missions trip.

My first and last trip was to Portugal. Even though it was very short—that's when I saw it. Poverty. I wasn't the *only* kid who grew up poor, homeless, and illiterate. There were literally hundreds of thousands of kids all around the world who needed help.

In Portugal, I got to help families living in Refugee Camps from Mozambique. It wasn't until I stepped foot out of the concrete jungles of New York City that I realized I am *not* a country boy.

Even though I lived in Staten Island, I still considered myself a Brooklyn boy, remember? Even though I grew up on the streets, I prided myself in being clean. The kids smelled like they hadn't bathed in months. I couldn't handle it man.

I struggled with not being able to speak the language. Setting up shelters wasn't my thing either. I realized during those two weeks that my heart burned more for New York and the inner city kids.

I didn't have to leave New York to be in full time ministry. There were kids like me without a home and family who needed my help. That was when I knew. My calling wasn't overseas missions—it was in my own backyard! It was a great feeling to know where I fit.

Next, I asked God to place me where the need was greatest. I appreciated that the pastors let me pick their brains any time. As a new Christian I needed this. I didn't find out how important it was until they suggested I join Prison Fellowship, a ministry of Chuck Colson. That's where I began to see how God could use my story.

With every opportunity, I shared with those who would listen that I should be dead or in jail for the rest of my life. It was then I realized how powerful my testimony was. It was electric to see God grab a hold of a person while I was speaking.

I served in a few prisons in New York City and Staten Island. I shared my story with a lot of guys who thought they were beyond saving. I told them if God could save me and give me a new beginning—then they could experience a new beginning too. I could be the example they needed to change.

I always made it a point to share there was a reason why I never got caught. I never missed an opportunity to tell them Jesus loved them like Otto told me many times.

Let me tell you something man. I love watching grown men cry. No story or person is beyond saving. There's something so humbling and sacred watching God change the most hardened heart.

Nothing is impossible with God.

A few years later, the pastor of our church was approached by David and Don Wilkerson of Times Square Church. They wanted to know if there were any Hispanic couples who were willing to join a three year internship program with Pastor Ben Padilla to start a youth program at The Challenge Center. We would be working *in* Brooklyn, and *in* the park where I used to get high.

I knew that was God. We prayed about it and accepted right away.

The first night we showed up, there were eight kids and their parents assembled. Immediately this kid named Dolly stood out. She was Puerto Rican. Her chair was directly in front of this African American kid who kept kicking the back of her chair.

Dolly was *not* having it.

The moment I hesitated to speak, Dolly filled the silence with her booming voice.

Kick my chair one more time, she said.

Kick.

Before I could say anything—Dolly was on her feet in a flash. She hit him in the jaw so hard that she knocked him out of his chair.

Bang! she yelled.

I'll never forget that moment. It's forever burned in my mind. With everyone looking at me, I quickly walked over to assess the situation, and to see if he was hurt.

Excuse me, I said. *I bet you won't kick the chair again.*

I laughed.

I couldn't help myself. The tension in the room was so thick that I *had* to cut it with my laughter. It was wild man. That was the start of an amazing bond we made with Dolly, and the rest of the families assembled. Growing up, our daughter Krista, was always surrounded by kids in the program. We grew the program to over a hundred kids and their parents.

The Challenge Center was where my passion for youth ministry ignited. If prison ministry was the vehicle, then youth ministry was the gas.

I was on fire.

I always enjoyed leading Sunday School with Nancy, and the opportunity to start a youth program was *the* thing I needed to find my fit in God's kingdom.

Ephesians 2:10 says, "For we are God's masterpiece. He has created us anew in Christ Jesus, so we can do the good things he planned for us long ago" (NLT).

Doing God's work as a new believer was so important. That is when I began to see the specific work He had planned for me to do.

MAY GOD BLESS YOU AND FAVOR YOU

When our three year internship with The Challenge Center in Brooklyn ended, I wasn't sure what to do next. I enjoyed being in ministry. I was working full time in a print shop, and had been with Dean Whitter printing for a few years. Financially we were doing okay, but I knew God still had work for me to do. But where, with whom, and for how long—I wasn't sure of yet.

While we were still at our church, we became good friends with David and Rebecca Biedel. We knew them when we were volunteers in the high school ministry. When they left to plant a new church called New Hope Community Church, we decided to check it out.

We loved it there.

We were there for a couple of years when Pastor David challenged me to quit my job with Dean Whitter and come on staff full time as their Youth and Family Counselor. Even though I didn't have any formal training, Pastor David felt God wanted them to bring me on as a pastor at New Hope. In addition, they helped me to become a licensed minister through the Christian Missionary Alliance in association with New Hope Community Church.

To this day, I don't know anyone on Staten Island—and maybe even all of New York—who loves Jesus more than Pastor David. I appreciate everything Pastor David did for me.

Becoming a pastor was the next right step for my family and I. Full time ministry changed my life and my family, but I always felt stuck in neutral. Prison ministry led to The Challenge Center, which led to becoming a pastor.

After I got saved, I told God that I didn't want to forgive my father. Although I had asked Nancy's father Nacho for forgiveness—this was way more difficult. I believed if you fool me once—shame on you. But if you fool me twice—shame on me.

I am not a fool.

My dad did many evil things to me as well as to the rest of my family. As a new believer, I knew what the Bible said about forgiveness (see below).

> *Matthew 6:14-15 says, "For if you forgive other people when they sin against you, your heavenly Father will also forgive you. But if you do not forgive others their sins, your Father will not forgive your sins."*

> *Matthew 18:21-22 says, "Then Peter came to Jesus and asked, 'Lord, how many times shall I forgive my brother or sister who sins against me? Up to seven times?' Jesus answered, 'I tell you, not seven times, but seventy-seven times.'"*

I knew I was supposed to forgive my father—but I couldn't. I couldn't bring myself to forgive my dad for the monstrous atrocities he caused. I believed if I forgave him that it would let him off the hook for everything he'd ever done. I was bitter. But I knew the verses from Matthew didn't lie.

I had just attended a conference on forgiveness when my mother called to tell me about my father. It was winter time. He was opening up a window to his apartment to let some of the heat out. As he was standing there, he had a brain aneurism. He fell down unconscious behind the sofa and landed with his face and shoulder on top of the radiator.

My sister went to visit my dad. When he didn't answer the door, she called someone from housing to let her in. That's when she found him lying unconscious. He was there burning for three days until she found him.

My dad was in a coma. He was in the hospital and wasn't expected to survive. I knew my mom's calling wasn't a coincidence. If I was going to forgive my father—now was the time. But I wasn't ready yet. I didn't know if I'd ever be ready. I struggled all day.

Should I go to the hospital? He never came to visit me in the hospital. Why should I visit him?

I made up a thousand and one excuses as to why I shouldn't go.

I finally went to the hospital in the evening. When I got there, I ran into my brother and sister. We all went upstairs together. It wasn't so much that I didn't want to go to the hospital, as much as I didn't want to forgive him. I didn't want to forgive my dad even though I knew what the Bible said.

In Puerto Rican culture, it's culturally appropriate to say *Bendicion* to your elders, which simply means *Bless me*. In return, they say, *Que Dios te bendiga y favoresca*, which means *May God bless you and favor you*. Culturally, not to say *Bendicion* to an elder is the ultimate insult.

That was the first thing my sister said when she saw my dad.

Papi. Bendicion, she said.

Bendicion, she said again. Instantly my father woke up.

Que Dios te bendiga y favoresca, he said.

We gasped.

I was shocked.

Tell him about me because he's going to die and go to hell, I felt God say to me.

Why don't you chop down every tree on earth and send it down to hell to make the fire nice and hot for my father? I said back to God.

The same hell You want me to send all those trees to make it nice and hot for your father—is for you too. The only reason you're not going is because of Me.

God had spoken. Twice. I was undone. When I started talking to my father, I couldn't stop. I told my father that I forgave him for what he did to me and the family. Then I shared Jesus with Him.

I gave my father an invitation. I told him to move his head or his hand if he wanted to accept Christ into his heart. He moved his hand. Right then I knew God answered my prayers. Minutes later my dad slipped back into a coma and died later that night. We buried him the next day with the dignity he *never* gave us.

The day I forgave my father I felt an incredible weight lift off my shoulders. If I thought God removing the monkey of drugs off my back was a giant weight—*this* was the ultimate weight. I never felt so much freedom in Christ and in my ministry as a pastor.

I was pleasantly surprised to learn that forgiveness wasn't just for the other person—it was for me first, and then my father! My heart agonized so much over the previous twenty-five years. He never lost sleep over what he did to me, but I certainly did. I experienced many sleepless nights thinking about my father and how he could do such evil things. How was I just supposed to forgive this man who used to beat me? Who threw my mother out of a window? Who fathered many children around the world? I finally let go of all the bitterness I held against my father.

I'm so glad I forgave my father. I'm so glad I went to the hospital. In my heart, I believed God is a God of miracles and that He loved to surprise us. I believe I will see my father in heaven someday.

This is the part of my story that I enjoy telling most because God set me free. He gave me a breakthrough. But I needed to learn how to forgive my father before I could continue the work He had for me. Please take a few minutes and answer the questions below, before moving on to Chapter 8 in *It's A New Beginning: How to Turn Setbacks Into Comebacks.*

QUESTIONS
1. Have you ever been surprised by God? Why? About what?
2. Do you believe God has work specifically designed for you? Why or why not?
3. Is there anyone God is asking you to forgive right now? Write their name down, forgive them in your heart, and pray for God's direction.

CHAPTER 8: BREAKTHROUGH

The day I forgave my father felt like God took His hand and shifted my life out of neutral into first gear, then second gear, and third. Things were happening. I had gifts. I was moving forward. I was ready to pay it forward to help others with the same help I received from God.

2 Corinthians 1:3-5 says, "All praise to the God and Father of our Master, Jesus the Messiah! Father of all mercy! God of all healing counsel! He comes alongside us when we go through hard times, and before you know it, he brings us alongside someone else who is going through hard times so that we can be there for that person just as God was there for us. We have plenty of hard times that come from following the Messiah, but no more so than the good times of his healing comfort—we get a full measure of that, too" *(MSG).*

First, I couldn't think of a more deserving person to help than my wife, Nancy. I kept my promise to her father Nacho. I promised Nancy I would send her back to school when our girls were old enough.

While I was the Youth and Family Counselor at New Hope Community Church, I put Nancy through college. She graduated with a Bachelors Degree in Social Work from the College of Staten Island.

Nancy found a great job through the city as a social worker. She loved working with families like I did at the church. It was around that time, I asked the director of the United Activities Unlimited gym across the street from the church to start a basketball league.

He rejected me.

He said it was because of the separation of the church and state. I knew better. Most of the kids who lived in the projects on Staten Island at the time were Hispanic and African American.

Thankfully, I didn't have to wait long. Soon after, the director informed me that the UAU was losing their funding. They wouldn't be able to keep their doors opened.

I came up with Plan B.

I knew George McGovern, the Chaplain of the New York Giants. We met at an inner city conference earlier that year. I asked the director to let me bring in nine New York Giants players for a city-wide event on *the* day the donors were visiting. This way, the donors would have no choice but to say *yes* to funding the gym again.

He agreed.

Before the event, I made a deal with him. If the donors came through on the funding, he'd have to give me the gym to start my basketball league. If not, he was off the hook.

We had over eight hundred kids. It worked! The event went off powerfully. The gym was immediately funded, and I got my league.

Twice a week, I hosted basketball games at the UAU for the kids in the projects. When they showed up, I immediately set the tone. If a player cussed once, they had to sit out of the quarter. If they cussed twice, they were thrown out of the game. However, they could play in the next game. Before each game I gave a twenty minute devotional. If they didn't come to the devotional, they couldn't play in the game.

These kids needed leadership. They were quick learners though, and learned the drill real quick. Over the next couple years, we grew the league to four teams with sixty players, including their girlfriends and family members.

It was during one of the pre game devotionals that a player's grandfather, who was eighty-nine years old, responded to the message. He gave his life to Christ right there in the middle of the gym. If that wasn't enough, the director became a Christian too.

The basketball league was growing. We asked a church in the area, Salem Evangelical Free Church, if they would let us use their facilities. The said *yes*. Their gym was much larger. We were able to use the gym more than twice a week. As a result, our sports ministry turned into something much more than twice a week games to reach out to the youth in the community.

My life was going great. My family was happy and healthy. My job at the church was making a difference in the community. Nancy was working full time as a social worker. Although I loved being a pastor, I couldn't ignore a stirring feeling like God might have work for me to do elsewhere. I spoke to my friend, Glenn Klenick, of Here's Life Inner City about what was going on, an he offered to pay for Nancy and I to fly to Fort Collins, Colorado. Every summer Campus Crusade for Christ—now called Cru—trains their staff on the campus of Colorado State University. They host rally's at Moby Gym with encouraging speakers from all over the world. We prayed and accepted his gracious offer. When we got there, I was surprised to reconnect with George McGovern, the Chaplain of the New York Giants, New York Yankees, and the New Jersey—now Brooklyn—Nets.

We clicked.

Once again, I remembered how much I enjoyed working with him at the UAU. Sports ministry was already a natural fit for me. The more I learned about all the ministries, including Here's Life Inner City, the more I knew Athletes in Action was the perfect fit for me. To this day, Glenn gives me a hard time about reimbursing him for the trip!

In order to join full time at Athletes in Action, I would need to raise support. Nancy would have to quit her job as a social worker. The job she worked so hard to get after completing four years of college. I knew it was risky. We knew it would take some getting used to. Not to mention that we were used to collecting a regular paycheck. This wasn't my second, or even my third job. It felt a little awkward to ask people, churches, and ministries to support us personally.

What kept me going during those few years raising support were the kids. I knew I would be able to reach them through the ministry of Athletes in Action in a way I couldn't reach them while working at the church.

I was that kid who slept in the park at night, and got high during the day. I knew sports ministry was the ticket these kids needed to hear about Christ's love in a way they'd never heard before. They needed to see there was life outside of the urban ghetto they called their home.

After three years of trying to raise support unsuccessfully, I came to my breaking point. This was not working. I couldn't raise enough money to join staff full time. Through a series of tough conversations, and much grace on both sides—Athletes in Action changed their support raising policies for people like me. Instead of raising support as full time staff for the whole family—I was an hourly employee. As an associate staff, I only had to cover the cost of my salary. Nancy kept her job as a social worker, and covered the cost of insurance for our family.

I was able to raise money for the things I cared most about like special sports projects for the youth in the community. I supplemented my income with speaking engagements at local churches, youth ministries, and men's events.

Without my knowledge, George McGovern heard me speak at a local church. He called me when he was going out of town, and wasn't able to speak at the New York Yankees Chapel service. He asked if I would speak. I was floored.

Yes. I would be honored, I said.

I shared my story, and it went very well. The next time George wasn't able to be there, he called me again. When George asked me to be his assistant to the New York Yankees, New York Giants, *and* New Jersey—now Brooklyn—Nets, I said *yes*.

Only in my wildest dreams could I imagine God opening up all kinds of doors. All I had to do was share my story with others. God was more than generous with me. He did the rest. Not only did I allow God to turn my setbacks into comebacks, He broke through my own limited understanding to help me see just how big He was. The more I allowed God to use my story, the more He blessed *me*. I believe when God wants to bless *you*, you didn't have to look for it—it will find you.

Friends, there's no halo on my head. No wings on my back. I have my buttons. We all have our buttons. I knew my story was special, but I had no idea that I would end up speaking to the New York Yankees.

They didn't pay me.

It was because of my affiliation with Athletes in Action and Baseball Chapel that I was able to speak to the players. It took faith and a lot of guts to quit my job at the church. I ended up where God wanted me—as a Chaplain's assistant to George McGovern—because I was bold and courageous.

Joshua 1:9 says, "Have I not commanded you? Be strong and courageous. Do not be afraid; do not be discouraged, for the Lord your God will be with you wherever you go."

THE BIG BREAKTHROUGH

God was always with me. Looking back, I am grateful to Prison Ministry for teaching me the value of sharing my story with others. That every story mattered.

If I thought leaving my job at the church for full time ministry was a new beginning—I was in for an even bigger surprise!

I like baseball, but I love basketball. I'm a basketball nut. When George turned the Nets over to me full time, I was quick to give glory to God. I was very intentional how I interacted with the players. I let them know that every single person was special. I told them their story mattered because God doesn't make junk.

I bonded right away with the coach, Byron Scott. He was a Christian who worked very hard to get the Nets back on track. During the 2003 season, the Nets had superstar talents like Jason Kidd and Alonzo Mourning. The Nets signed Alonzo to a four year contract, but quickly retired months later with kidney disease. His cousin, Jason Cooper, was a great match for a kidney transplant.

After the surgery, Alonzo was sick. Really sick. He was dying. I remember God telling me to go to the hospital and visit him. I was scared to death. I didn't want to go.

Alonzo was a *very* private player. Every time I saw him in the locker room or on the court, I said *hello*. Most of the time, he rarely acknowledged me.

When I hesitated to visit him in the hospital, I heard God speak to me.

Just go, He said.

So I went.

Pastor Willie, How are you doing? He said with a smile.

I was surprised. I told Alonzo I didn't expect to get past the door, his bodyguard, or even have a long conversation with him. We chatted for a while. He told me more about his condition, and how his kidney transplant went.

I told him the real reason I showed up.

I get that you're almost dying, and you don't mind being with the pastor—so let me ask you a question Zo. What are you going to do with God? Where do you stand with God?

Then, I told him my story. I explained why I asked him what I did. I told him that I'd done so many bad things in my lifetime. I never thought God would forgive me.

That's when Alonzo said he wanted to give his life fully over to God.

I was floored.

Then Alonzo got better. Much better. After Alonzo got out of the hospital, he became like my spiritual son. He worked hard to fully recover and return to play in the NBA with the Miami Heat.

His life long dream was to win the National Championship. When the Heat made it all the way to the finals, Alonzo flew Nancy and I to Miami to watch him play. Alonzo Mourning won the NBA Championship with the Miami Heat.

It was surreal man.

It seemed like yesterday when I sat next to his bed in a New York hospital. Shortly after winning the championship, he wrote a biography called *Resilience*. I was honored he mentioned me in his dedication. If you read Chapter 10, you'll read all about our friendship.

That fact that God would put me in a position to influence this superstar of superstars was crazy. The fact that Alonzo would write a book, put my name in the dedication, and take a chapter out of his book for me—blew my mind.

That's insane!

Only God could do that. On my best day, I couldn't put that stuff together.

Alonzo was inducted into the NBA Hall of Fame, and he flew Nancy and I to be there with him to celebrate. During his acceptance speech, I about fell out of my chair when he mentioned my name.

I told Alonzo, the only way you ensure a big breakthrough or comeback was to get right with God. To allow Him to speak into your life. To mold you. To send men and women into your life to help you like God did with me. When you allow yourself to do that, you put God in a posture to bless you.

God blessed Alonzo Mourning in a big way. God blessed me in an even bigger way for sharing with Alonzo. God showed *His* love for *you* by going to the cross. We show we love God by the way we live.

We don't come to the Lord to look like other people. The world celebrates superstars. It tries to create a melting pot concept. They like to melt you down to have you come out looking *just* like them—like all the other superstars.

Be your own star. Don't let them do that.

I don't look like anybody, and I don't want anybody to look like me. Can you imagine two Willie's walking around in New York City? That would just be weird man.

You don't need to become closed-minded either. Just make sure that you're living a righteous and holy life!

Discipline. You have to discipline yourself. I don't want to bring death to myself or the ministry God gave me with Athletes in Action. I don't want to shame my children like my father either.

I'm a wretched dude man. If I let the old Willie come out, there's going to be a problem. If I come to the Lord like everything's going to be alright—that's baloney.

> *Philippians 2:12-13 says, "Therefore, my dear friends, as you have always obeyed—not only in my presence, but now much more in my absence—continue to work out your salvation with fear and trembling, for it is God who works in you to will and to act in order to fulfill his good purpose."*

It took me *y-e-a-r-s* to work out my salvation. To understand that God could forgive someone like me. I had to get to a place where I was confident in what God had done in my life to share it with others like I did with Alonzo Mourning.

CHAPLAIN WILLIE ALFONSO

I believe a life worth living takes work. You get in what you put out. I preached at the New York Yankees chapels for five years before I asked Mariano Rivera to help me start a chapel for the Spanish speaking players.

According to Major League Baseball officials, 27.1% of its players are of Hispanic background, and 28% of MLB players were born outside of the United States.[4] That's a lot of players who weren't hearing the message of the gospel in their native tongue.

Mariano Rivera is Panamanian. I'm Puerto Rican.

I believe God wanted me to ask Mariano *why* they didn't have Chapel in Spanish. I told him that I would love to start one. I figured if he was on board, who was going to say *no* to him?

Nobody.

James 4:3 says, "You do not have because you do not ask God. When you ask, you do not receive, because you ask with wrong motives, that you may spend what you get on your pleasures."

All I wanted was to share the same comfort God gave me. I'm so glad I asked Mariano—because he got the permission we needed to move forward. We started a Chapel in Spanish for the New York Yankees. Now that we had permission, I found myself with a serious problem. My Spanish was horrible!

What have I gotten myself into? I asked Mariano.

I'll bail you out any time you mess up, he said.

Luis Sojo helped too. He used my not-so-good Spanish as an opportunity to make a joke. This helped to lighten things up. They both guided me. They helped me tremendously. My Spanish was getting better and better without a problem. God sent these men into my life to get me to where He wanted me to go.

God has consistently given me a way out. When George McGovern saw the success of the Spanish Chapels, and the bonds I was creating with the players—I became the Chapel leader for the New York Yankees Spanish Chapel full time. From time to time, I speak at the English speaking Chapels as well.

Right after that, I became the Chapel Leader with the Staten Island Yankees—a Minor League Baseball team. I hosted Spanish and English speaking chapels for them as well.

For the past fifteen years, I've had a one on one Bible Study with Mariano Rivera at his house. We've became like brothers. Of course, it doesn't hurt that he is the *greatest* closer pitcher in the history of baseball. We had a Bible study with the guys at his house. His wife, Clara, cooked wonderful meals, and we'd sit and have the time of our life.

Friends, real men the Lord. Real men stand up and pray for one another. Real men change. They don't stay the same.

Today, Clara is the senior pastor of Refuge of Hope. She is one of the most godliest women I've ever met. The Rivera's restored a one hundred and seven year old building where they now host services for the community.

One of my most favorite verses on change that I love to share whether I'm speaking at Baseball Chapel or at a church is from Ezekiel 46:9.

> *"When the people of the land come before the Lord at the appointed festivals, whoever enters by the north gate to worship is to go out of the south gate; and whoever enters by the south gate is to go out the north gate. No one is to return through the gate by which they entered, but each is to go out the opposite gate."*

No one is to return the way they entered. Did you catch that? Loving the Lord will change you. It will *not* make you a punk. I was a punk before I met Christ. He changed me. Thank God I didn't return the same man I came in as. That junk didn't work anymore.

I don't walk around with a fifty pound Bible. I just want God to use my story. If God can use me to bring comfort to others, why would I keep it to myself? God has turned all my setbacks into comebacks. That's my calling. To share His love with others. To share how He can change you.

Friends, you don't have to stay the same anymore. The old has gone the new has come. Don't you see it?

Isaiah 43:19 says, "See, I am doing a new thing! Now it springs up; do you not perceive it? I am making a way in the wilderness and streams in the wasteland."

Do you know where God wants you to go? It's not easy to walk through difficult times. Believe me. It's easier to skip to the good parts of your story. It doesn't work that way. Before God blessed me with the big breakthrough, I had to learn discipline and work ethic. Please take a few minutes and answer the questions below, before moving on to Chapter 9 in *It's A New Beginning: How to Turn Setbacks Into Comebacks.*

QUESTIONS

1. What is your story? Have you ever shared your story with others?
2. Have you ever quit a job to pursue a dream? Why or why not?
3. What does discipline mean to you? Why? How has it helped you?
4. Have you ever asked God for a big breakthrough? Why or why not?

CHAPTER 9: HOW TO TURN SETBACKS INTO COMEBACKS

T he choices you make determine where you go. Ask any athlete that I've worked with what my favorite quote or saying is—and I guarantee that the word *choices* is in there somewhere. Our thoughts lead to every day choices that become life long habits. An athlete isn't born overnight. A superstar doesn't become a star without lots of practice in their particular field.

The day my mom kicked me out of the house at age eleven changed *e-v-e-r-y-t-h-i-n-g*. Suddenly, I was the *only* one making choices for myself. I didn't have anyone to look out for me. At an age when kids should only be concerned with picking their friends or what to wear for school—I was forced to fend for myself.

It was rough man.

I don't know how I survived all the setbacks. I lost a part of my soul every time my father beat me. My home wasn't safe. When my parents turned their back on me, I found solace in the streets. I turned to drugs when I felt I had no other choice. I smoked pot to get high to forget the pain of my past. I was just a kid growing up Brooklyn. No matter where I went, trouble followed me.

I couldn't catch a break.

I was not dreaming of the future when I met Nancy. It just happened. She saw straight through my tough exterior. She was the first person who ever loved me. I felt like I was living a fairy tale, and I didn't believe in that stuff.

Nancy gave me hope. When her love didn't silence the voice of marijuana, I went back to drugs. Harder drugs. I was so angry at the world when I met Gus Sosa and Sally Walker at Sterling's High. They showed me kindness. They cared for me when nobody else did. They said I could be somebody.

That my life mattered.

Otto Lang told me the same thing. Over and over, he told me that *Jesus loved me.* I rejected Otto. I rejected His Jesus. Many times I thought I had reached the end of my life. It wasn't until I heard God's voice one Saturday night that I woke up.

I could die. My family was going to leave me. It wasn't until I reached my breaking point that I asked for help. Otto brought me to church. Christ did the rest. God revealed parts of me that no one else knew. He exposed my sin and shame. Instead of exploiting my weakness—He gave me a way out.

I was offered a choice. For the first time in my life, I saw where hope lies. In Christ, I was given a new life. A future and a hope.

> *Jeremiah 29:11-13 says, "'For I know the plans I have for you,' declares the Lord, 'plans to prosper you and not to harm you, plans to give you hope and a future. Then you will call on me and come and pray for me, and I will listen to you. You will seek me and find me when you seek me with all your heart.'"*

I was given a new beginning. The day I forgave my father freed my heart. I wasn't bitter anymore. I had a bright future. God gave me a second chance to be the husband and father I knew I could always be.

Only in my wildest dreams did I see myself going back to the same place where I thought I blew it. He gave me opportunities to help the kids in the park—the same park I used to get high.

Only God could take my failures and use them for something good. Only God could take my story and use it to influence people on professional teams like Alonzo Mourning and Mariano Rivera. Like the players on the New York Yankees, Staten Island Yankees, and Brooklyn Nets.

CHOOSE FOR YOURSELF

Loving the Lord won't make you a punk. Loving the Lord will change you. It will change your whole life. I believe God wants to change you like He changed me. I believe He wants to give you ten comebacks for every setback. But you have to want it. You have to choose for yourself. Just like God made me choose the night I stepped foot in church.

Romans 3:23 says, "For all have sinned and fall short of the glory of God."

All have sinned. Everyone has experienced setbacks. I'm not the only one. It's because of God that all of my setbacks have turned into comebacks. Not just any sized comebacks, but God-sized comebacks. The kind with my name on it.

I believe God has specific work designed for me and for you. No matter how many mistakes you've made, God is offering you another chance.

A new beginning.

If you would like to make the choice to become a follower of Christ like I did, like Nancy did three days later, say this prayer with me.

Say it out loud.

Dear Jesus,

I acknowledge my sin before you. I confess my anger, pride, sin and shame. Please come into my mind and clean up my thoughts. Come into my heart and make it new. Take my heart of sin and make it soft to receive Your Words. Help me to become the person You created me to be. Show me the good works you have for me to do—only I could do. Thank You for listening. Thank You for hearing and answering my prayer. Thank You for coming into my heart and making me whole. Take whatever monkeys are on my back and remove them. Once and for all, help me to serve you. Today, I choose You Jesus. I choose life. Thank You for loving me and forgiving me of my sin. Amen.

Welcome brother! Welcome sister! Your name is now written in heaven. You are now part of the family of God. I encourage you to get into a Bible believing church. There is no such thing as lone ranger Christians.

One of the things I had to learn after becoming a Christian was how to keep walking through all the hurt and the pain. Just because you give your life and heart to Jesus, doesn't make things suddenly easy. You can't point your finger at anybody but yourself.

I am living proof that you can overcome the irresponsible decisions of others. I've experienced many disappointments and personal tragedies.

Maybe you're struggling to forgive the mistakes of others—or maybe you're trying hard to forgive yourself. Either way, you have to choose for yourself.

Deuteronomy 30:19 says, "This day I call the heavens and the earth as witnesses against you that I have set before you life and death, blessings and curses. Now choose life, so that you and your children may live.

I hope you choose life. Not just for your sake but your children's sake. Child abuse is unacceptable. Children have rights too. I am living proof that you can survive, but no child should have to go through what I did. I don't believe God wants battered women to stay in abusive relationships. It bothers me that many women are told by the church to let God figure it out. That God hates divorce. He does. But, he also hates abuse. We are so busy telling women to stay in dangerous situations. But what about the women who get out?

We forget to praise the women who leave. We don't talk about the women who refuse to put up with that junk. The women who don't stay. The women who choose life for themselves and their children. Who take a stand and refuse to let their kids inherit the generational curse.

I am an advocate for children's rights. I believe that God doesn't want any women or children getting their teeth kicked in physically or emotionally. I also believe there are just as many women and children who are being emotionally abused, and need the courage to say *no*. To ask for help. To get out.

While writing this book, I didn't want to miss out on an opportunity to make a statement. To speak from my heart. I've been working with the youth of New York and New Jersey for the past forty years. Forty years! It breaks my heart when I see broken families continuing the cycle of violence. No child should have to endure abuse like I did.

I have suffered much abuse in my life time. Not just from my own family and those who abused me, but from the church. I meant it when I said that preachers who preach that everything's going to be alright when you come to Jesus is a straight up lie. It's baloney.

I experienced so much hurt after I became a Christian. I realize I'm touching some taboo topics, but I had to speak up. There were a few churches and ministries who hurt me. Who took advantage of me. But, if my life can be a catalyst for someone else, then so be it.

Every time a setback knocked me down, I got back up. If one church didn't fit right, I found another one. If there's *one* thing you take away from this book let it be that we will all experience setbacks. They will come. They will knock you down. It's inevitable.

Please don't let hindrances stop you from pursuing the Christian walk. There's nothing God's love and the love of His people can't see you through.

One of my favorite Psalms is Psalm 23. It says,

> *"The Lord is my shepherd, I lack nothing. He makes me lie down in green pastures, he leads me beside quiet waters, he refreshes my soul. He guides me along the right paths for his name's sake. Even though I walk through the darkest valley, I will fear no evil, for you are with me; your rod and your staff, they comfort me. You prepare a table before me in the presence of my enemies. You anoint*

my head with oil; my cup overflows. Surely your goodness and love will follow me all of the days of my life, and I will dwell in the house of the Lord forever."

Friends, let's continue walking. Did you catch that? It says never to stop. Continue keeping your eyes on God.

I know a lot of people who have experienced hurt from their pastor or the church, and they walked away from God. What I said to them, and I will say to you—is don't let those things hinder you. It's part of the walk.

I began attending Christ Tabernacle after being hurt badly by some Christians. I didn't allow those people and those things to move me away from God or the church. Pastor Michael and Maria Durso encouraged me. They invested in me like Gus Sosa, Sally Walker, and Otto Lang did.

Their church has such an anointing. Just being there is such a blessing. For the past ten years, Nancy and I have traveled an hour from Staten Island to Queens and back just to be there every Sunday. The commute and the sacrifice paid off because I found a son in Pastor Ralph Castillo.

What I'm trying to say is that you have to find the right church. Everyone needs to get connected. A lone ranger is dangerous for a reason. In the end, we discover that God is the mastermind.

There's a story in the Bible about a people group known as the Israelites who faced the toughest choice. It wasn't about choosing the impossible. No! They had already crossed the Red Sea.

To the Israelites, this choice didn't seem as difficult. I believe that's why God put this passage in Scripture. Often times we are most at risk when we don't feel like our choices matter. They do. When making the choice doesn't seem like a big deal. It is.

Joshua 24:15 says, "But if serving the Lord seems undesirable to you, then choose for yourselves this day whom you will serve, whether the gods your ancestors served beyond the Euphrates, or the gods of the Amorites, in whose land you are living. But as for me and my household, we will serve the Lord."

The Israelites had to make a choice whom they would serve. I had to make that choice. Sooner or later, you will have to make the same choice.

I told God that if He took the monkey of drugs off my back that there would be no one who would serve Him more loyally than me. I've kept my promise even though it's been one of the hardest choices I ever made.

What about the Israelites?

If you've read the story of the Exodus, you know that God was no longer providing a pillar of fire by night and cloud by day. There was no more free food on the ground, literally called manna or *what is it?*. It was time to make a choice. Move forward or die. They had to make a choice.

What about you?

Have you ever felt stuck so bad that you needed a new beginning? I don't want to intimidate anyone, but I can't stay silent. I'm so glad I didn't let the narrative of my life choose for me. Setbacks are not the end of my story. Setbacks are not the end of your story. I don't believe you can out give God. I believe in the saying, *a work for everyone and everyone at work.*

IT'S A NEW BEGINNING

I should be dead right now. I should be dying of AIDS somewhere. I should be doing life in jail, but I'm not. I've been raising support for the past twenty years with Athletes in Action and I've never gone without. I'm now in my sixties serving God and loving others.

Romans 5:8 says, "But God demonstrates his own love for us in this: While we were still sinners, Christ died for us."

Nancy and I started a foundation in 2007 called It's A New Beginning (IANB), which is also the title of my book. I made the easy choice to give back. For every comeback I was given, I decided to pay it forward. Whether you have a little to give or a lot to give—you give out of the abundance of your heart because Jesus loves you. I had to learn that man. When Nancy and I started a foundation in 2007, I did not want *self-made* to be a part of our vocabulary. No one is *self-made* because we believe no one makes it without help and encouragement along the way.

Every staff member, volunteer, mentor/mentee and donor understands that we are what we are and have what we have because at strategic junctures of our lives, someone came along to lend a hand, share advice or help create a new opportunity. Through mentoring, scholarship and education, It's A New Beginning continues to pay it forward.

Gratitude is the driving force of our foundation. Where would any of us be, if it wasn't for prayerful and thoughtful individuals creating and supporting opportunities to make our lives better.

Today if you are struggling to find a new beginning—your new beginning—I challenge you to give your heart to God. Join a Bible believing church and get involved. Pay it forward. Give back to those who have given to you out of the kindness of your heart.

Today if you would like to know more information about my ministry or to learn more about the foundation, please go to WillieAlfonso.com or ItsANewBegining.org. There you can learn the many ways to get connected, attend various events, or support the ministry with tax-deductible donations.

I can't say this enough man. Thank you for reading this book. Thank you for reading my story. Let me pray for you:

Dear God,

I pray for my brothers and sisters. I pray for Your goodness to overwhelm them. I pray, Lord God, that You would give them at least ten comebacks for every setback they've experienced in life. I pray that You would bless them with a new beginning. With new life. With new relationships. I pray, Holy Spirit, that You would speak to them. Show them that You are the Way, the Truth, and the Life—and that no one comes to the Father except through you, God. I pray my life would be an example. No life is too messed up. No setback is too much to overcome. Thank You God that You are a God of comebacks. You are a God of miracles who loves to surprise Your children with good things. May every good and perfect gift come from You. May it not disappoint. Thank You for loving them when no one else does. Prove your love to them today. Help them to choose your love, in Jesus' name. Amen.

Setbacks don't have to be the end of your story. I believe God wants to bless you with more comebacks than setbacks. It is my prayer that, after reading my story, you will choose for yourself. *What are you going to do with God? Where do you stand with God?* Please take a few minutes and answer the questions below, in *It's A New Beginning: How to Turn Setbacks Into Comebacks.*

QUESTIONS

1. Have you made the choice to become a follower of Christ? If not, it's not too late. Read the prayer on page eighty six, and ask God to change your life. If so, rejoice that your name is already written in the Lamb's Book of Life (Revelation 21:27).
2. What or whom are you currently serving with your time and money? Are you paying it forward?
3. Do you need a new beginning? Ask God to give you a future and a hope today.

SMALL GROUP DISCUSSION QUESTIONS

If you would rather answer the questions in a book club or small group, feel free to use the questions at the end of each chapter listed here instead.

Chapter 1: Growing Up Brooklyn
1. Where did you grow up?
2. What was your family like? Home life?
3. Do you have any sad childhood memories? Happy? Why or why not?
4. At what age did you become a man or a woman? What happened?

Chapter 2: That's *Your* Son!
1. Have you ever stolen? Why or why not?
2. Have you ever done drugs? How old were you when you started?
3. Were you ever hurt by a family members actions growing up? What happened?
4. What's the worst thing anyone's ever said to you?

Chapter 3: The Day I Became Nancy's Partner
1. Did anyone take a chance on you when you were young? If so, who and why?
2. Have you ever experienced love at first sight? Why or why not?
3. Who or what makes you want to become a better person?
4. Who was your father figure growing up? Why?
5. Do you remember how old you were when you believed "you can become something" in this life?

Chapter 4: Love and Basketball
1. Have you ever lived a double life or felt like a hypocrite? Why?
2. What's your favorite sport to watch? To play? Why?
3. What do you think is worse: loving someone deeply and losing them, or never loving at all?

Chapter 5: Going to the Chapel
1. What was the best thing that ever happened to you?
2. What makes you feel inadequate?
3. Have you ever been welcomed into a new family or been kicked out of because of something you said or did?
4. What is your number one fear and why?

Chapter 6: The Day I Met Otto Lang
1. Have you ever met anyone who was the *real* deal? How did you know they were who they said they were? Why?
2. Have you experienced a breaking point? If so, who did you turn to? Why?
3. Have you ever come to a point in your life where you can say with confidence that Jesus loves *me*? Who was the first person you told, and how did they respond?

Chapter 7: The Day I Forgave My Father
1. Have you ever been surprised by God? Why? About what?
2. Do you believe God has work specifically designed for you? Why or why not?
3. Is there anyone God is asking you to forgive *right now*? Write their name down, forgive them in your heart, and pray for God's direction.

Chapter 8: Breakthrough

1. What is your story? Have you ever shared your story with others?
2. Have you ever quit a job to pursue a dream? Why or why not?
3. What does discipline mean to you? Why? How has it helped you?
4. Have you ever asked God for a big breakthrough? Why or why not?

Chapter 9: How to Turn Setbacks Into Comebacks

1. Have you made the choice to become a follower of Christ? If not, it's not too late. Read the prayer on page eighty six and ask God to change your life. If so, rejoice that your name is already written in the Lamb's Book of Life (Revelation 21:27).
2. What or whom are you currently serving with your time and money? Are you currently paying it forward?
3. Do you need a new beginning? Ask God to give you a future and a hope.

NOTES

1. *Merriam-Webster OnLine*, s.v. "dysfunction," accessed March 26, 2015, http://www.merriam-webster.com/dictionary/dysfunction.
2. *Good Reads*, s.v. "John Wayne," accessed April 1, 2015, https://www.goodreads.com/author/quotes/45481.John_Wayne.
3. *Metro Lyrics* s.v. "Smokey Robinson," accessed April 28, 2015, http://www.metrolyrics.com/ooo-baby-baby-lyrics-smokey-robinson.html.
4. *2014 Opening Day Rosters Feature 224 Players Born Outside the U.S.*, accessed June 12, 2015, http://m.mlb.com/news/article/70623418/2014-opening-day-rosters-feature-224-players-born-outside-the-us.

ABOUT THE AUTHOR

Willie was born and raised in Brooklyn, New York, the product of an abusive and alcoholic father. At the age of ten he was forced to leave home when his mother chose to turn him away after he defended her during a beating from his then crazed and drunken father.

Willie spent his teenage years living with relatives, friends and on the streets of Brooklyn. He turned to drug use early on and continued destructive habits into his young adult years. In 1972, at the age of seventeen, he married his wife Nancy and continued to abuse drugs until Palm Sunday, 1981 when he received Jesus Christ as his Lord and Savior.

In 1996 he and his wife felt called into full-time, inner city ministry. Willie began working with teenagers in a sports ministry where hundreds of young people came to Christ. He now serves as Chaplain to the Brooklyn Nets and Chapel Leader for the Staten Island Yankees and the Hispanic players of the New York Yankees. Willie continues to reside on Staten Island with his wife Nancy. They have three daughters, Venus, Yvette and Krista, and two grandchildren, Julie and Jonathan. Connect at WillieAlfonso.com.

Made in the USA
San Bernardino, CA
15 October 2018